Social Accountability SA8000

The First Decade

SOCIAL ACCOUNTABILITY SA8000 THE FIRST DECADE

Implementation, Influence, and Impact

EDITED BY
DEBORAH LEIPZIGER

Viva Books

New Delhi | Mumbai | Chennai | Kolkata | Bangalore | Hyderabad | Kochi | Guwahati

First Indian Edition 2010

VIVA BOOKS PRIVATE LIMITED

- 4737/23 Ansari Road, Daryaganj, New Delhi 110 002
  E-mail: vivadelhi@vivagroupindia.net, Tel. 42242200
- 76, Service Industries, Shirvane, Sector 1, Nerul, Navi Mumbai 400 706
  E-mail: vivamumbai@vivagroupindia.net, Tel. 27721273, 27721274
- Jamals Fazal Chambers, 26 Greams Road, Chennai 600 006
  E-mail: vivachennai@vivagroupindia.net, Tel. 28290304, 28294241
- B-103, Jindal Towers, 21/1A/3 Darga Road, Kolkata 700 017
  E-mail: vivakolkata@vivagroupindia.net, Tel. 22836381, 22816713
- 7, Sovereign Park Apartments, 56-58, K. R. Road, Basavanagudi, Bangalore 560 004
  E-mail: vivabangalore@vivagroupindia.net, Tel. 26607409, 26607410
- 101-102 Mughal Marc Apartments, 3-4-637 to 641, Narayanguda, Hyderabad 500 029
  E-mail: vivahyderabad@vivagroupindia.net, Tel. 27564481, 27564482
- Beevi Towers, First Floor, SRM Road, Kaloor, Kochi 682 018, Kerala
  E-mail: vivakochi@vivagroupindia.net, Tel: 0484-2403055, 2403056
- 232, GNB Road, Beside UCO Bank, Silpukhuri, Guwahati 781 003
  E-mail: vivaguwahati@vivagroupindia.net, Tel: 0361-2666386

www.vivagroupindia.com

Published by arrangement with

Greenleaf Publishing
Aizlewood Business Center,
Aizlewood's Mill, Nursery Street
Sheffield S3 8GG, UK

ISBN: 978-81-309-1476-3

Published by Vinod Vasishtha for Viva Books Private Limited, 4737/23, Ansari Road, Daryaganj, New Delhi - 110 002. Printed and bound by Anand Sons, Delhi - 110 092.

Contents

Foreword

Partha Sengupta
Vice President Corporate Services and SA8000 Management Representative,
Tata Steel Limited, India

The social accountability movement in its first ten years is coming of age just as the world learns and unlearns ways to address the many challenges facing us in the pursuit of peace, prosperity, and security in the midst of rapid change.

In our journey of a hundred years of excellence and emergence as the world's sixth largest steel producer, some facets of Tata Steel have remained constant. These have much to do with the way we perceive our larger purpose and our belief that growth must be attained not by any means, but guided by ethical and sound business principles of integrity, understanding, excellence, unity, and responsibility. The notion of social stewardship is integral to our business endeavors in areas where we operate. Ethics and responsibility are interwoven in the daily course of Tata Steel business and, directed by corporate policies and our Code of Conduct, extend to our stakeholders as well.

It is with these aspirations toward standardization, continual improvement, and innovation, and to enhance our legacy of labor practices implemented within the company ahead of the law of the land, that Tata Steel approaches SA8000. The Social Accountability Policy, which came into effect in 2003, marks a paradigm shift in how we understand our corporate commitment. While, up to this point, we had looked at our own responsibility toward our stakeholders, we are now guided to *positively influence our partners to do their share for their stakeholders*. Tata Steel aims to engage especially with suppliers and vendors in ensuring workplace rights and dignity for all who associate with us either directly or throughout our supply chain.

Today we may be among a handful of large corporations in this part of the world in demanding in very explicit language the basic workplace conditions of our partners for their employees, sub-contractors, and so on, and as such a cultural exception for those we engage. Yet I believe we have made positive progress in this direction. In time to come, the ripple effect of this small step in an otherwise long journey will lead like-minded enterprises to join in and create a larger social wave that lifts the quality of life in our communities.

We in Tata Steel, the flagship enterprise of the Tata Group, in the second century of our existence, have the opportunity to work with diverse communities and stakeholder groups in the 26 countries where we are represented. SA8000 is an implementation tool in our vision: *to be a global benchmark in value creation and corporate citizenship.*

In being called upon to write the foreword to *SA8000: The First Decade*, I wish the movement continued success going forward.

Introduction

Open-eyed management

Alice Tepper Marlin
President, Social Accountability International, United States

John Tepper Marlin
Principal, CSRNYC, and Adjunct Professor, New York University Stern School, United States

As we survey the trail of government and business errors that have laid waste the global economy, this book provides an important message. At the heart of recent failures of capitalism was a disregard for past laws and conventions plus blind faith in the phony magic of black boxes marked "trust me." These black boxes hid unprecedented risk, fraud, and deceit. The end of illusion has meant a worldwide suspension of trust.

This book offers a way out of the maze of mistrust in the job-anxious world of post-illusion 2009. It is about a sustained effort by high-minded but practical people to develop and implement global standards in multi-stakeholder meetings that are inclusive and open. It is about managers, workers, and community leaders working together on hard-nosed management and performance systems to implement real improvements in the work lives of people the world round. This book is about practical problems and clear-eyed solutions.

There is no magic about the procedures described in this book, but there is magic in the process and the outcomes when people undertake it with sincere commitment. Implementing a decent work standard and redesigning human resource systems can transform workplaces, enabling workers to produce the same volume of output during normal working hours, and ending excessive overtime. Workplaces can be made safer, workers can become more confident that their voices are being heard and their concerns addressed, and managers can see the bottom-line benefits.

This book is important because it provides real-life stories, factory by factory, of how these workplaces have become more humane and more productive. Executives will find inspiring examples of how workplace improvements can accrue to the bottom line. Consumers will find ways to buy from brands, retailers, and producers working hard to eliminate sweatshops and child labor. Governments will find a culture of compliance with their labor laws, enabling them to more efficiently deploy their enforcement resources. Workers will find practical ways to improve the quality of their work life.

As the current deep recession continues to bring tighter credit, budget cuts, and lay-offs, some ask: "In these times, is a responsible workplace an unaffordable luxury? Must such a lofty goal for the time being be given up?"

By and large, programs for decent work and environmental improvement do not seem to have taken more than their share of the pervasive cuts. Yes, companies have cut back on spending for corporate social responsibility (CSR) programs, just as they have other aspects of their business. But the goal of reaching higher labor or environmental standards and the relevant tools seems at long last to be regarded as intrinsic to business plans and operations.

U.S. President Barack Obama's first steps have been intensely focused on creating jobs and improving the environment. He wants to create five million new U.S. green jobs. Yet he is also concerned about environmental goals and labor conditions all over the world. The employers and brands in this book are doing their part, showing by example how companies can prosper while advancing step by step to reach and meet both legal requirements and additional aspects of Social Accountability 8000 (SA8000), such as basic needs wage and a management system.

SA8000 is still a very young standard, with the resource limits of youth, but also the advantage of vigor and the goodwill of a broad extended community of stakeholders.

Voluntary standards were established because governments alone seemed unable or unwilling to assure decent work on a global basis. Clearly the private and the public sectors need to work together to reach this goal. Guides that rate corporate cultures and achievements, such as *Shopping for a Better World* (Tepper Marlin *et al.* 1988), have had demonstrated impact. Consumers have begun to respond to CSR labels that they trust. Coffee shops increasingly sell ethically traded coffee. Consumer response to the "No Dirty Gold" campaign spurred the jewelry and mining industries to undertake significant new programs. Recent studies by Harvard Professor Michael Hiscox show that consumers offered real online choices among tee shirts or coffee beans will pay a 15–25% premium for those that are labeled ethically traded or SA8000. Voluntary programs are no substitute for government regulation, but they can play a crucial supportive role, fostering a "culture of compliance." The International Labour Organization, the UN's oldest agency, has embraced voluntary standards with its "Decent Work" program.

This is the time to implement voluntary company standards. The time for a book like this has arrived.

So it is an honor and a pleasure for us to introduce this feast of stories that together say loud and clear that the SA8000 workplace standard is improving the lives of workers. One million people work in fully compliant facilities (independently verified). Millions more are in facilities that are seeking compliance to the standards. Some management teams in nearly every country choose to do so simply because of the reputational and bottom-line benefits. Others respond to the efforts of global brands that are members of Social Accountability International (SAI)'s Corporate Programs to recognize and reward improvements, especially certification to SA8000. Still others are among the 240-plus retailer members of the Business Social Compliance Initiative of the Foreign Trade Association of Europe step-by-step program and tools. Some of the most far-reaching approaches to scaling up are innovative public–private initiatives, partnered by standard setters, ministries of labor, development agencies, trade associations, unions, employers, and non-governmental organizations.

This practical, easy-to-read book is written primarily by practitioners themselves:

Executives report on a variety of ways in which they approach the same overarching goal of implementing the SA8000 standard. A clothing retailer like The GAP Inc has a different challenge from a fruit grower like Chiquita. Gucci and TNT have quite different supply chains and business models. Yet they all require and develop messages that will reach and motivate their management staff and the workers who produce their goods and services. Their reports show that they implement in different ways, based on different philosophies, pursuing different journeys, and facing varied challenges and constraints. Yet all of these companies are making progress that amply demonstrates their substantial commitment. Their stories show how flexible the SA8000 standard can be, as implemented in retail stores, in factories, on banana farms, and in delivery services. And they show that the journey can be as important as the destination.

Industry associations have a major role to play in the all-important mission of scaling up. Individual company case studies provide inspiring examples, but true progress is achieved when entire industries embrace the standard, in cooperation with their stakeholders. In Europe, more than 220 retailers (supermarkets and hypermarkets) are working through the Business Social Compliance Initiative to evaluate their suppliers against SA8000 (their "best practice"), then step by step to remedy deficiencies.

Researchers are finding out how SA8000 helps companies perform. For example, in workplaces where other management system standards are already in effect, the addition of SA8000 has been found to reinforce the management system in place and cut implementation costs. A group of faculty members led by Michael Hiscox, Clarence Dillon Professor of International Relations at Harvard, are seeking better ways to evaluate the effectiveness of standards and certification programs. They call for measuring outcomes and facilitating comparisons by introducing control groups and increasing sample sizes. They have begun research on the impacts at a Central American garment factory implementing SA8000, with technical assistance from SAI.

Trainers are developing curriculum materials and books for disseminating the SA8000 standard. Deborah Leipziger and Rossella Ravagli are among those who have led the way with books. At SAI, Doug de Rouisseau, Craig Moss, Martin Ma, Judy Gearhart, Jane Hwang, Eileen Kohl Kaufman, and Elena Arengo have contributed mightily to developing a wide range of training programs and documents such as the SA8000 Guidance document.

This book speaks in the voices of practitioners themselves, describing how SA8000 is implemented on-site, how the monitoring tools are used, and how third-party certification makes the job of supply-chain management easier and more transparent.

The writers cover:

- Implementation at a single company
- Implementation in the supply chain to a brand
- Industry-wide scaling up in a shared stepwise program
- Government as a partner and beneficiary

Professor John Ruggie in his report to the United Nations is impatient with the speed of the implementation of voluntary standards, urging voluntary programs to get up "to scale" and governments to step in to issue incentive plans and/or regulations. The International Social and Environmental Accreditation and Labelling (ISEAL) Alliance has published a set of informative case studies on government advancement of voluntary standards.

In many ways this book is a landmark. This is the first time a voluntary social standard celebrates its first decade, providing a wide range of experiences and lessons learned. A great deal has happened since Deborah Leipziger first published *SA8000: The Definitive Guide to the New Social Standard* in 2001.

With her wealth of knowledge on codes of conduct and social standards, Ms. Leipziger is the ideal editor for this book. Deborah has been involved in SA8000 since its creation, guiding the original process that led to its creation, and observing the first pilot audits and its implementation in Europe, Asia, and Latin America. In her capacity as adviser to many social standards and guidelines, companies, and UN agencies, Ms. Leipziger places the first decade of SA8000 in perspective.

Thank you, Deborah Leipziger.

Alice Tepper Marlin and John Tepper Marlin
January 25, 2009

References

Leipziger, D. (2001) *SA8000: The Definitive Guide to the New Social Standard* (London: Financial Times Prentice Hall).

Ravagli, Rossella (1999) *Guida Pratica sulla Responsabilità Sociale* [*Practical Guidance on the Social Responsibility*] (SGS Training Center & De Qualitate, October 1999).

Tepper Marlin, Alice, *et al.* (1988) *Shopping for a Better World* (New York: Ballantine Books).

Part 1
Implementation

1

TNT and SA8000

Mike Patrick

TNT Express

Background

In 2003, TNT recognized the importance of market differentiation to ensure its survival in a highly competitive market. Demonstrating leadership in corporate sustainability was one part of our strategy to achieve overall industry leadership. We also recognized that corporate social responsibility (CSR) encompassed not only what we did with our profits, but also how we went about making them. We said that it went beyond philanthropy and compliance to addressing how we managed our economic, social, and environmental impacts, as well as our relationships with our stakeholders.

A key part of our CSR strategy is to actively engage in stakeholder dialogue. There are two main reasons for this. First, stakeholder dialogue provides a vehicle for obtaining information on key issues for stakeholders and, where discrepancies or issues arise as to current policy, for entering into discussions on possible solutions. Second, taking into account the reputation of the transport sector, we believe that, if our business is able to enhance our reputation among stakeholders, then we will automatically enhance our own reputation (and that of our sector?).

TNT is above all a service organization. This means that the motivation and well-being of our staff are critical to our operations and our ability to deliver a differentiated service to customers. Engaging employees in corporate sustainability was considered an opportunity to instill pride and genuinely inspire them, in particular in commitments that extended beyond compliance.

Actively seeking new ways to help the world opens the door to new and innovative initiatives. This has a positive impact on our employees and drives their willingness to operate at the peak of their abilities.

In November 2001, our Chief Executive Officer, Peter Bakker, was reading an article during a flight to Singapore. It quoted the appalling statistic that a child dies from hunger every few seconds. Bakker says:

> It also noted that there was enough food in the world for everyone. It's just that we're not getting it to the places where it's needed most. That got me thinking that hunger is essentially a logistics issue on a global scale. It seemed to me that TNT was in a unique position to be able to make a contribution to solving this problem. In our company we have the skills, systems and people that could do something to help.

In December 2002, the United Nations World Food Programme (WFP) and TNT launched a ground-breaking partnership aimed at a single common goal: fighting world hunger. It was called "Moving the World."

Kofi Annan, the former United Nations Secretary-General, made the following comment: "The partnership between TNT and WFP is an excellent example of the way private corporations can cooperate with United Nations agencies to do vital life-saving work."

TNT aims to manage its business with respect for its impact on society and the environment in all the communities in which it operates. Ultimately, this means taking its share of responsibility by doing all it can to preserve and improve the world for future generations.

More than anything else, we want to be a well-respected and trusted organization that demonstrates accountability not only to customers and shareholders but also to our employees and the world at large. Since 2002 we have started to integrate our sustainability initiatives and approaches to ensure that our policies and practices effectively reflect our vision. We now have a clearly defined three-step approach toward sustainability:

1. We are implementing various international standards in order to retain our license to operate

2. We aim to enhance our sector's reputation by engaging in stakeholder dialogue and by implementing sector key performance indicators

3. We measure, benchmark, and report on our performance, and we lead the industry by initiating unique commitments, beyond compliance

Our approach is to progressively implement these goals throughout our business areas. We recognize that the key to success in sustainability is the willingness to take responsibility and to be accountable for everything we do.

This was stated in our first Corporate Sustainability Report in 2004. A key part of our reporting is transparency about our progress. So the 2004 report formed the basis from which we continue to improve both our reporting and our impact on the world in which we live. Our mission statement includes the following key aspects of our approach to CSR:

- Our mission is to exceed customers' expectations in the transfer of their goods and documents around the world

- We deliver value to our customers by providing the most reliable and efficient solutions in distribution and logistics

- We lead the industry by
  - Instilling pride in our people
  - Creating value for our shareholders
  - Sharing responsibility for our world

TNT wanted to demonstrate its commitment on three levels. Our approach can be thought of as a three-stage pyramid shown in Figure 1.1, with our standards at its base, industry-related initiatives in the middle, and TNT's unique approach to sustainability at the top.

We also wanted to build sustainability into our business processes, so we recognized that reporting against the Global Reporting Initiative (GRI) would help us develop when refining our data and reporting systems for our future reports.

So what did we mean by "manage"? By the end of 2007 we wanted 100% coverage of the management systems throughout fully owned operations, so this meant achieving Occupational Health and Safety Advisory Services (OHSAS) 18001, International Organization for Standardization (ISO) 9001 and 14001, Social Accountability (SA)8000 (for countries outside the

FIGURE 1.1 TNT's commitment to CSR

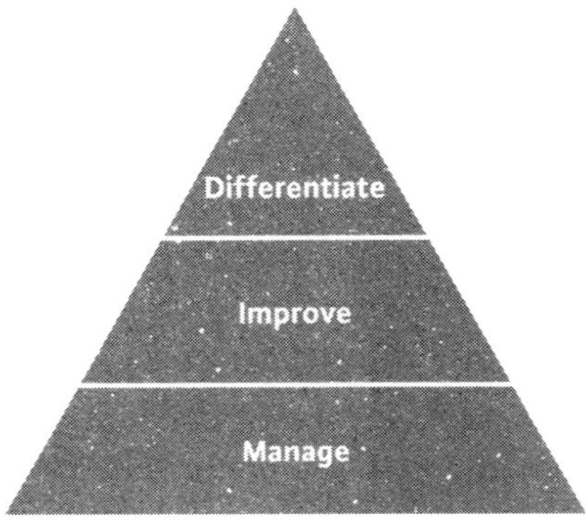

Organization for Economic Cooperation and Development [OECD]) and Investors in People standards.

TNT also had growth ambitions to continue to move into non-OECD countries such as Brazil, China, India, and Russia. Globally, in the non-OECD countries, we wanted to comply with the standards of various regulatory agencies such as the United Nations, the International Labour Organization (ILO), and the World Bank.

Acquisitions were also part of our growth strategy. We wanted to be in a position to ensure that newly acquired TNT entities also adhered to our social responsibility policies and practices.

FIGURE 1.2 Management: the standards

Management: the standards		
Manage	Meet corporate governance code	
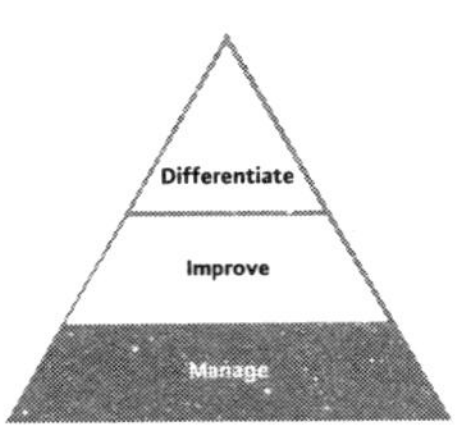	Ensure operational excellence	ISO 9001
	Ensure a safe place to work	OHSAS 18001
	Ensure a responsible impact on our world	ISO 14001
	Enable people to grow	Investors in People
	Demonstrate social responsibility	SA8000*
	Report our sustainability performance	GRI
	Status: sustainability standards to be implemented within three years in fully owned operations. * Compulsory in non-OECD countries	

TABLE 1.1 TNT stakeholder dialogue since 2004: results

The results show substantial difference between top five expectations from each of the stakeholder groups. Despite the variation, there is clear agreement that the dominant concerns are compliance with legislation, social aspects, and reducing emissions.

Civil society 2004	Customers 2004	Subcontractors 2005	Employees 2005	Investors 2005	Suppliers 2006	Customers 2006/07
Reducing CO_2 emissions	Compliance with legislation especially where enforced weakly in developing countries	Child labor in the supply chain, especially second and third tier	Increasing alternative fuels and energy in vehicles and buildings	Reducing environmental footprint	Compliance with legislation especially where enforced weakly in developing countries	Employee health and safety
Employee health and safety including HIV/AIDS	Child labor in the supply chain, especially second and third tier	Compliance with legislation especially where enforced weakly in developing countries	Accountability and transparency relating to strategy and management decisions	Assuring security and safety of transportation	Reducing CO_2 emissions	Reducing CO_2 emissions
Pollution associated with vehicle particulates	Compliance with code on social issues	Anti-competitive behavior associated with price-fixing and profit implications	Pensions and retirement benefits for employees	Achieving recognized excellence by customers	Discrimination: equal fair treatment of all employees	Fair and reasonable terms of employment
Community health and safety including HIV/AIDS	Implementing environmental management systems	Reducing CO_2 emissions	Compliance with legislation particularly where enforced weakly in developing countries	Implementing good governance and risk management	Accidents in the workforce: driving and in warehouses	No child labor
Partnerships with local and international organizations	Continuous improvement in environmental performance	Bribery, corruption, and conflict of interest	Ensuring good work–life balance as essential to well-being and quality of life	Implementing international codes of conduct and labor standards in globalized operations	Bribery, corruption, and conflict of interest	Compliance with legislation

We recognized that recent years had seen a rapid growth in public sustainability reporting, and also the feedback we have been receiving from dialogue with our stakeholders had identified certain trends, as Table 1.1 shows.

Our approach to CSR seeks to encompass strategies and practices that aim to meet the needs of stakeholders while seeking to protect, support, and enhance the human and natural resources that will be needed in the future.

Our next step in the process was to conduct global risk assessments to further confirm and establish the types of mitigating actions that we need to put into place (see Table 1.2).

Table 1.2 TNT Express: top ten corporate sustainability risks 2006

Risk	Ranking (top 10)	Type of risk	Mitigating actions
Environmental pollution (noise and air), fuel leakage, or pollution/ storage of bulk fueling and their impacts	1	Environ-mental	Implementing ISO 14001 globally as well as specific policies and training programs on noise, air quality, fuel leakage, and storage. All are internally and externally audited to maintain the standards
Not complying with local legislation (e.g., aviation security, child labor, maximum working hours, minimum wages, vehicle emissions, etc.)	2	Social Environ-mental	Competent people are employed. Internal controls and processes have been identified. Global social policies and standards have been set and agreed. All are internally and externally audited to maintain the standards
Child labor within TNT workforce, subcontractors, or suppliers	3	Social	Global social policies and standards have been set and agreed. Supply-chain management processes have been developed and implemented. All are internally and externally audited to maintain the standards
Increasing undeclared dangerous goods	4	Social	Dangerous goods advisers in all locations. Sales people have training in dangerous goods. Systems and procedures are in place and checks are carried out at all locations

continued over →

Risk	Ranking (top 10)	Type of risk	Mitigating actions
Supplier and subcon- tractors not supporting TNT views and conduct (e.g., child labor, poor H&S, fatal accidents, ethical behavior issues), impacting TNT reputation	5	Social	Environmental and social accountability aspects incorporated in procurement processes, which also include risk assessments. This ensures that staff, customers, and suppliers know TNT's minimum requirements
Employees/subcon- tractors/owners: drivers exceeding legal working hours/working hour regulation	6	Gover- nance Social	Policies and procedure are in place and working hours are tracked within TNT HR functions. Working hours requirements are also identified as part of the procurement procedures
Environmental restrictions, i.e., delivery in city centers, use of clean vehicles, driving at night	7	Environ- mental	Compliance with local requirements. Currently piloting and using electrical vehicles in inner cities. Community surveys are used and all complaints are recorded and acted on
Employing illegal immigrants/workers	8	Social	Recruitment processes and procedures are in place that check all new recruits
Not complying with TNT public commitments, specifically on CSR goals and objectives	9	Gover- nance	There is a working party and a CSR department that monitors the goal and objectives and ensures key performance indicators are in place
Increasing fatal accidents	10	Social	Road-safety management system and driver and manager training programs implemented. Key performance indicators are in place to track and report on the effectiveness of the program

The board of management's commitment to CSR moved us forward very quickly and led to the following statement in our 2004 CSR report: "For most companies, the essence of sustainability seems to be avoiding liabilities—not doing bad things. For us, sustainability is our ongoing search for opportunities to actively do good things and then report on our progress."

Our CSR policy came very soon after and demonstrates the level of commitment from all our board members (see Fig. 1.3).

FIGURE 1.3 TNT CSR policy

TNT Corporate Social Responsibility Policy

Our aspirations

TNT is a global business that strives to improve its social and environmental impact on communities around the world. We aspire to help people realise their potential and to meet the needs of the current generation without producing a poorer world for our children by compromising the ability of future generations to fulfil their own needs. To meet these aspirations towards our stakeholders, we subscribe to the United Nations Global Compact, which embraces, supports and enacts a range of values in the areas of human rights, labour standards and the environment that we can influence.

The quality of our footprint on local, regional, national and global societies is a key factor when communities decide whether to extend their consent to our operations in the long-term. TNT is developing and maintaining policies and practices that promote a positive and sustainable environmental and social contribution to every community in which we operate. The TNT Code of Business Principles underpins this commitment to legal compliance, continuous improvement and sustainability.

Our initiatives

TNT is undertaking a variety of initiatives to support our aspirations and values:

- Encouraging operating units to achieve international standards including Investors in People, ISO 9001:2000, ISO 14001, OHSAS 18001 and SA 8000.
- Training employees on the social and environmental dimensions of their roles.
- Encouraging our suppliers to introduce programmes that support our own objectives and targets because we take responsibility for the effects of our entire supply chain in line with the TNT Code of Business Principles.
- Benchmarking our policies, strategies and programmes internally and externally to encourage continuous improvement in all areas of our activities.
- Developing programmes that reduce the emissions of our operational activities.

Our communications

We are committed to communicating and building a dialogue with internal and external stakeholders about our challenges and accomplishments in achieving our sustainable development and environmental management goals.

Our internal award

We hold an annual competition to celebrate the best internal initiatives and results in the field of sustainable development and environmental management.

Public reporting

We will reflect our progress and future plans in our social responsibility report to enable all our stakeholders to understand and monitor our performance and future plans.

M.P. Bakker	C.H. van Dalen	H.M. Koorstra	M.C. Lombard
Chief Executive Officer	*Chief Financial Officer*	*Group Managing Director Mail*	*Group Managing Director Express*

TNT

Approach

We have a clear-cut sustainability strategy and we wanted to improve our performance as a responsible employer by implementing five management systems. These are OHSAS 18001 (health and safety), Investors in People (training and employee development), SA8000 (labor standards and human rights, in non-OECD countries), ISO 9001 (quality), and ISO 14001 (environment).

We saw the implementation of these systems as helping to ensure continuous improvement in our performance in these areas. Their implementation also provides us with clear key performance indicators, as well as evaluation and benchmarking processes.

In our road to social leadership, we developed our approach for internalizing our stakeholder feedback into our CSR strategy and so developed our approach on the five standards.

A key part of this was the application of SA8000 among our sites in non-OECD countries in order to guarantee compliance with UN and ILO codes on universal labor standards. This would also make our business unit and country managers advance in social accountability.

In developed countries (OECD), compliance with international labor standards (ILO) is covered in the aim of complying with national legislation. Because TNT has only recently started implementing SA8000, limiting coverage to non-OECD countries was felt the best approach and that we should conduct gap analysis in the OECD countries we operated in. (An exception is TNT Express Italy and Portugal, which achieved certification in SA8000.)

Journey and design

We started our journey in 2004 and agreed that our target for all the standards was 100% certification to the standards by December 31, 2007.

While we fully understood the health, safety, environmental, and quality aspects, we had not collectively put all the SA8000 elements together as an actual standard.

So our first step was to hold a two-day training program for the relevant internal and external stakeholders so that we could find out from the experts the content and approaches taken in the various countries.

TNT's global social accountability program was designed to:

- Ensure all our stakeholders were identified and involved
- Provide a system to meet the requirements of the SA8000 standard and the relevant stakeholders
- Identify the relevant legal requirements appropriate to our activities
- Ensure any other requirements to which the location subscribes are taken into account, including best practice and any local operational restrictions
- Document all employees' social accountability roles and responsibilities
- Provide a self-assessment process to develop a plan with identified responsibilities and timelines
- Identify and document elements of existing and proposed work activities that present a significant health and safety risk. (This is covered under OHSAS 18001)
- Outline how the social accountability objectives and management programs are to be set and monitored to improve performance
- Outline the documents, procedures, and instructions required to implement and maintain the management system
- Outline the training and competence required to control our social accountability program
- Facilitate planning, control, monitoring, corrective action, auditing, and review to ensure compliance with TNT's social accountability policies
- Provide direct global support through our divisional corporate social responsibility function

From these we developed agreed individual plans and support with the countries and business units. Our next approach was to develop a framework based on plan–implement–check–act (now often known as plan–do–check–act [PDCA]), shown in Figure 1.4.

This framework represents a comprehensive management information system that provides our business with tools for managing all of its social

FIGURE 1.4 Framework for sustainability in social accountability

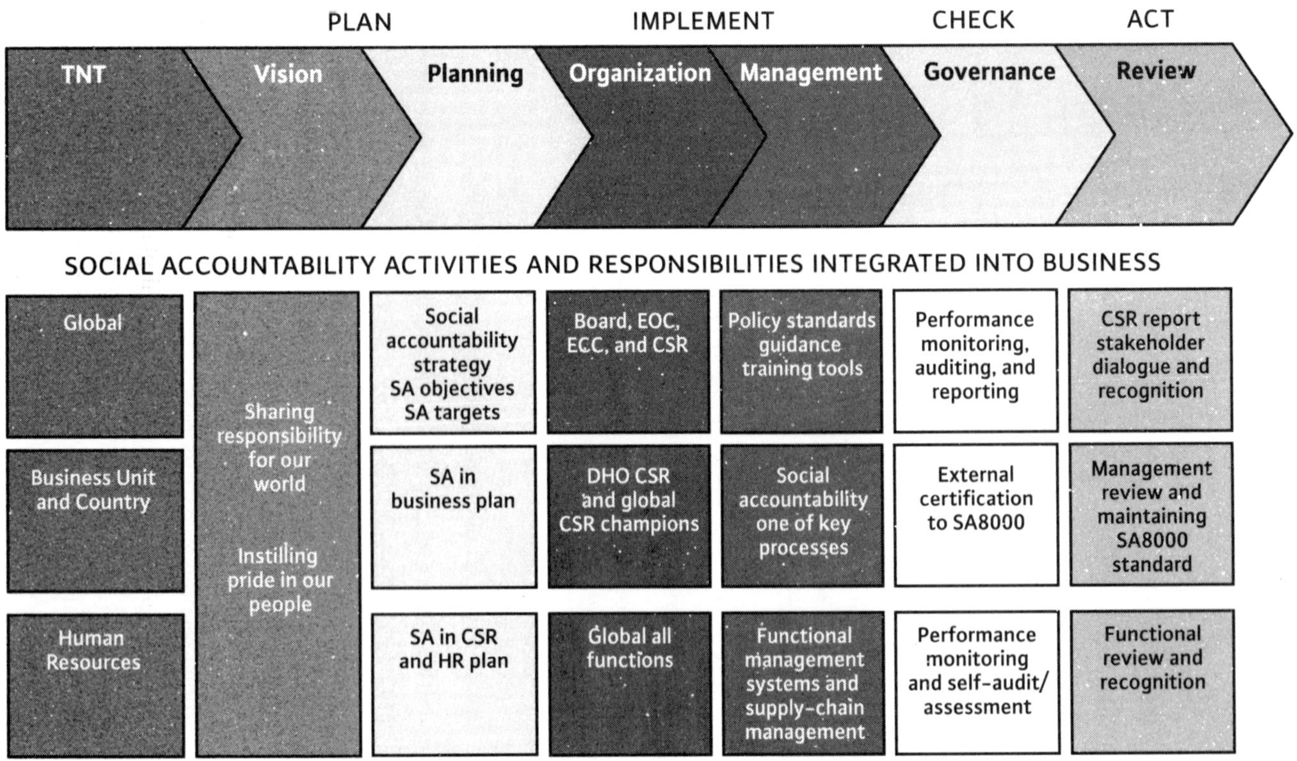

Key: CSR = corporate social responsibility; DHO= Divisional Head Office; EEC Express Executive Committee; EOC Express Operating Committee; HR = human resources; SA = social ac ountability

accountability responsibilities and measuring its progress through key performance indicators.

OHSAS 18001 takes care of the health and safety aspects, and the process for implementing this program used the same approach as for SA8000.

The management system framework is reviewed as part of the continual improvement process to ensure that standards are maintained and further enhanced.

Implementation

We have found that the core element of our management systems is the main and supporting policies, which give guidance in strategic day-to-day management decisions and actions. To be effective, all our policies had to address the root cause of the problem as well as being owned and understood.

Based on the self-assessment approach we were able to determine priorities and objectives for the implementation plan and for meeting the targets. We found that we had to be very careful with setting targets for achievement of the standard as the scope of social accountability extended beyond TNT premises and employees.

The various levels of maturity in the business units and countries did create some challenges, but it enabled us to learn from one implementation process and therefore to improve the next, and so on.

The implementation process had to be sustainable as well as meeting the requirements of the standard and demonstrate compliance to the certification bodies. This required continuously monitoring activities and results and, as this was for all five standards, it created quite a workload from a global perspective.

The level of commitment and support from the board of management through to the business units and countries made it easier but it also raised expectations. A key part of the TNT culture is our "sure we can" attitude and the willingness to self-correct, which placed a lot of pressure on the divisional CSR team.

TNT's targets stated that by December 31, 2007 we would certify our operation in 32 countries, which included Italy, China, Hong Kong, Taiwan, Mauritius, Argentina, Chile, Bahrain, Egypt, Jordan, Kuwait, UAE, Saudi Arabia, Namibia, South Africa, Bulgaria, Estonia, Finland, Greece, Israel,

Latvia, Lithuania, Portugal, Romania, Russia, India, Indonesia, Malaysia, Philippines, Singapore, Thailand, and Vietnam.

TNT achieved compliance with SA8000 and all of the other four standards by December 31, 2007.

Challenges

The main challenges came from:

- Local laws, particularly in regard to working hours
- Inconsistency of auditors
- Supply-chain management
- Custom and practice

There were a number of issues with certification auditors' approaches that ranged from misinterpretation of the SA8000 standard, to not understanding local law and regulations, to using standards from another country, to applying their own personal standards. Although in the main these were resolved, it did delay things and cause internal friction which could have been avoided. For example:

- The auditor told management that they should have casual labor standing in line outside the building in the event that someone goes off sick or when they had unusually high volumes
- The auditor told employees they should be asking for meal allowances

Supply-chain management was not only a challenge but also a key learning point as it involved addressing more demanding social and environmental expectations while striving to improve our business performance. While we did have robust systems in place, it did make us review our processes and:

- Recognize that our activities have a wider impact on the society in which we operate
- Take into account the economic, social, environmental, and human rights impact of our activities across the world

- Seek to achieve benefits by working in partnership with other groups and organizations

On custom and practice we found that if auditors were not from the country they did not always understand local custom and practice and, more importantly, how to deal with it.

Another challenge is the danger that any certification scheme may become a process of managing paperwork and documentation of evidence rather than a tool for changing behavior and culture. Our focus has therefore been on the sustainable processes, changing working conditions and behaviors, rather than on the endpoint of certification.

Conclusions

Knowledge of our stakeholders' concerns helps us to develop new products and services as well as to address social responsibility challenges in cooperative ways. It is also increasingly acknowledged by mainstream investors and rating agencies as indicating good operational and risk management.

We also recognize that an important part of our commitment was, and still is, sharing responsibility for the world in which we operate and that sustainable development is a process of continuous change meeting the present and future needs of the business.

Globalization has heightened our sense of responsibility and interconnectedness.

We began our stakeholder dialogues in 2004 as part of the World Economic Forum (WEF) Logistics & Transport Corporate Citizenship Initiative (L&TCCI). This ongoing cross-industry initiative allows us and other members to work together in identifying and developing potential solutions to those issues that affect a range of stakeholders.

One of the first pieces of work undertaken by the L&TCCI was to identify which stakeholder groups are important to the logistics and transport sector. We identified the following key groups: customers, civil society, suppliers, subcontractors, investors, and employees.

After identifying these groups, the L&TCCI asked an independent corporate citizenship consultancy to consult with customers, civil society, suppliers, and employees during 2004 and 2005. The main benefit to TNT was the development of a comprehensive stakeholder questionnaire that has enabled us to take into consideration our stakeholder concerns in our CSR strategy.

There have of course been some benefits and also some ongoing challenges. Some of the benefits that TNT has seen are:

- Increase in employee confidence in sharing issues and expressing their opinions freely
- Employees' perception that SA8000 has resulted in tangible benefits to them
- Increase in employee-engagement results[1]
- Enhanced CSR image, particularly in countries where TNT is the only company with the standard
- Better understanding of and focus on the supply chain
- Better transparency and understanding of local custom and practice
- Consistency in performance

Some of the challenges in certain countries are:

- Staff attrition due to the containment of overtime
- Hiring of temporary workers who may not be competent
- Increased base costs

We have developed and implemented a global supply-chain engagement process that incorporates our social values and business principles and the steps we have started to put into place to work together on meeting these values and principles.

1 High results from our annual Employee Engagement Survey reflect the positive impact that corporate sustainability is having on the pride of employees. Comparison with benchmark data (from 41 companies and 360,000 employees) demonstrates above-average performance:

- 79% are "proud to work for TNT" compared to 64% from the benchmark
- 80% rated TNT as "socially responsible in the community" compared to 65% from the benchmark
- 75% believe "TNT is an environmentally responsible company" compared to a benchmark of 72%
- 61% have "been involved in supporting TNT's partnership with the United Nations World Food Programme through donations in time and/or money"

Our approach is to encourage and work with our suppliers to introduce programs that support our own objectives and targets because we have to take some responsibility for the effects of our entire supply chain.

The current global business environment is motivating organizations to consider the full social and ethical impacts of their corporate activities and policies. Those companies that are able to demonstrate a responsible approach to broader social and ethical issues will gain a vital competitive edge and inspire the confidence of their stakeholders.

TNT recognizes that standards and social auditing process can help to ensure worker and citizen rights in developing countries where regulations are weak and resources for enforcing them are limited, as well as assuring our stakeholders of consistency in our performance.

TNT recognizes that applying SA8000 or any other standard cannot in itself guarantee fair practice; it must be combined with continuous monitoring by our workers, management, NGOs, and local authorities as well as having "mind-sets" of social values that are not only espoused but also lived and owned by our business units and countries.

2

SA8000 in Tata Steel

Developing process-driven sustainability approaches

Priyadarshini Sharma
Tata Steel, India

Inspired by the belief that core areas and infrastructure could transform India, the Tata Group was constituted in 1868 by Jamsetji Nasserwanji Tata.[1] Pre-dating the "business case" and the triple-bottom-line rationale, financial outlays accompanied environmental and social investments for his dream of a steel mill and a community that would emerge as Tata Steel, Jamshedpur.[2] In its 101st year, Tata Steel's core values, group purpose, vision, mission, strategic goals, and policy framework mirror its

1 Tata, the 98-company multinational, was named the sixth most admired business house by U.S.-based Reputation Institute in its 2008 annual global 200 list.

2 "Be sure to lay wide streets planted with shady trees, every other of a quick growing variety. Be sure that there is plenty of space for lawns and gardens. Reserve large areas for football, hockey and parks. Earmark areas for Hindu Temples, Mohammedan Mosques and Christian Churches . . ." (Lala 1981: 14). These are the words of J.N. Tata in 1902, five years before the site of the steel plant was finally decided, in a letter to his son Sir Dorab Tata, describing what his dream city of steel should look like. The township of Sakchi was renamed Jamshedpur in 1919 by Lord Chelmsford as a tribute to J. N. Tata (1839–1904).

Box 2.1 About Tata Steel

Flagship of the $62.5 billion Tata Group (www.tata.com), Tata Steel (www.tatasteel.com) is the world's sixth largest steel company with an existing annual crude steel production capacity of 30 million tons per annum (mtpa). Established in 1907, it is the first integrated steel plant in Asia and is now the world's second most geographically diversified steel producer and a *Fortune* 500 company.

Tata Steel's Jamshedpur (India) Works has a crude steel production capacity of 6.8 mtpa which is slated to increase to 10 mtpa by 2010. Through investments in Corus, Millennium Steel (renamed Tata Steel Thailand), and NatSteel Holdings, Singapore, Tata Steel has created a manufacturing and marketing network in Europe, Southeast Asia and the Pacific Rim countries. Corus, which manufactured over 20 mtpa of steel in 2008, has operations in the UK, the Netherlands, Germany, France, Norway, and Belgium. Tata Steel's product offerings cater to automobile, construction, packaging, and engineering sectors and include: flats (hot rolled, cold rolled, and galvanized sheets); longs (rebars and high- and low-carbon wire rods); tubes; pipes; bearings; and hand tools and implements.

Tata Steel's vision is to be the global steel industry benchmark for value creation and corporate citizenship.

Tata Steel India is the first integrated steel company in the world, outside Japan, to be awarded the Deming Application Prize 2008 for excellence in total quality management.

sustainability journey. This case outlines Tata Steel's stakeholder-engagement enabling framework and discusses the implementation experience utilizing SA8000 as a component of its business sustainability strategy.

Corporate citizenship and stakeholder commitment

To become a global steel industry benchmark in value creation and corporate citizenship, the company continually works at improving its corporate governance compliance and adheres to the Tata Code of Conduct. Its inclusive growth model is realized in partnership with government, and national and international development organizations. A significant

Box 2.2 The Tata Steel Jamshedpur experience: toward inclusive and socially responsible industrialization

Healthcare, civic amenities, and community services in Jamshedpur

The company makes healthcare facilities available to employees and the community through an 890-bed hospital and 11 dispensaries, supporting allied hospitals and medical units, promoting health awareness (especially HIV/AIDS), alternative healing, and wellness. "Healthcare for all" is promoted through urban and local programs, and a unique effort is the Life Line Express, a railway train or a hospital on wheels, which has been taking medical aid to distant communities lacking such infrastructure since 1991.

Tata Steel, through its subsidiary, operates the Jamshedpur Township, maintaining roads, parks, gardens, a zoological park, supplying over 3.5 million gallons of clean water daily, providing emergency fire service, public health, and airport services.

Community initiatives

Tata Steel believes that it cannot prosper in isolation. Community services and social welfare initiatives started by the company since 1950s—Family Welfare Initiative Foundation (TSFIF) 1950, Community Development and Social Welfare (CD&SW) 1958, Tata Steel Rural Development Society (TSRDS) 1979—provide bottom-of-the-pyramid interventions in sustainable livelihood (agriculture, skills training, self-help group creation), health and sanitation, education, empowerment and environmental conservation, supporting vulnerable groups such as marginalized farmers, unemployed youth, women, children, and the differently abled.

portion of profits—approximately 5–10%—is annually pledged to initiatives that address wide-ranging needs identified in collaboration with local communities.

Policies of Tata Steel

Under the belief that intentions are effective only when they are clearly communicated, interpreted, and enacted in day-to-day life, the company has rolled out, over a period of time, its clear-cut stance on key concerns of stakeholders. In chronological order of enactment, the following are Tata Steel's intentions translated into action through formulation of policies to provide organizational direction:

- Quality policy
- Alcohol and drug policy
- HIV/AIDS control policy
- Human resource policy
- Corporate social responsibility policy
- Environmental, occupational health and safety policy
- Social accountability policy
- Affirmative action policy
- Research policy

Tata Steel's quality and sustainability enabling framework

Tata Steel has been implementing quality enhancement initiatives such as the Tata Business Excellence Model (TBEM),[3] Total Operational Performance (TOP), Total Preventive Maintenance (TPM), Value Engineering, Six Sigma, Customer Value Management (CVM), and Retail Value Management (RVM) to support its modernization plans since the 1980s. Consistent with a culture of continuous improvement, social aspects are important elements in achieving corporate excellence and regularly feature in assessments, verifications, and improvement efforts. Furthermore, the company integrates quality and sustainability practices in its strategic (policy) and routine (daily management) functioning as part of its Total Quality Management (TQM) implementation, increasingly extending the plan–do–check–act (PDCA) cycle to the intangible extra-financial business aspects. Tata Steel addresses stakeholder needs through specific

3 A group-wide award framework, the TBEM is adapted from the criteria of the U.S. Malcolm Baldrige National Quality Program.

standardized tools such as the International Organization for Standardization's ISO 14001 and ISO 9001, Occupational Health and Safety Assessment Series (OHSAS) 18001, and the more recent SA8000. Together, these constitute the company's corporate sustainability management system, facilitating the company's efforts to proactively develop policies, strategies, and measures to address concerns and needs beyond compliance to norms.

Inputs from stakeholders are taken through several structured formal and informal engagement processes and considered while setting strategic objectives for the company. Company vision, mission, and goals; national development agenda; customer needs; past performance and feedback; Tata Group guidelines; along with employee and stakeholder consultation processes constitute the organizational framework for formulating and implementing sustainability approaches and action plans. Annual business plans include community development, employee welfare, environmental management, occupational health and safety, and labor and supply-chain aspects. Actions on various issues are tracked through key performance indicators. Investor surveys, customer satisfaction surveys, employee satisfaction surveys, and community needs analysis are also undertaken periodically.

Pioneering labor practices

The first labor association came into being in India in Tata Steel in 1920 and the Tata Workers Union was born in 1937. Welfare measures not restricted to basic workplace amenities such as potable water, washrooms, canteens but including medical facilities, housing, sports, and leisure and recreation facilities have long been an integrated part of Tata Steel's industrial relations philosophy. Policies and practices in improving the quality of work and life of the worker were initiated within the company without the mandate of national legislation,[4] many of which went on to become law such as the eight-hour working day, worker compensation, maternity benefit scheme, and free medical aid (see Table 2.1).

4 K.C. Mehra, former Executive Director, Tata Steel (1985–97), in *Tata Workers Union Diamond Jubilee Commemorative Magazine*, 1982.

TABLE 2.1 Pioneering labor practices

Welfare activities	Date introduced by Tata Steel	Date introduced by law in India
Eight-hour working day	1912	1948
Free medical aid	1915	1948
Welfare department	1917	1948
Schooling facilities	1917	–
Works committees	1919	1948
Leave with pay	1920	1948
Workers provident fund	1920	1924
Workmen compensation	1920	1924
Technical institute	1921	1961
Maternity benefits	1928	1946
Profit-sharing benefits	1934	1965
Retiring gratuity	1937	1972
Ex gratia payment	1979	–

Some perspectives:

> There is a well-laid system of joint working and collective bargaining. Many other welfare measures are identified, discussed and implemented at various joint-working committees. Worker representatives are respected at all levels and encouraged to discuss various issues concerning production, productivity and welfare of people. [5]

> Tata Steel provides necessary support through management systems. Mere good intentions and well meant efforts are not sufficient to sustain good industrial relations. Professionalism and formal systems are insisted and agreed upon by both sides, and are codified and made known to workers and supervisors.[6]

5 S.N. Pandey, former Executive Director, Industrial Relations, Tata Steel, in *Tata Workers Union Diamond Jubilee Commemorative Magazine*, 1982.

6 R.C. Billimoria, in *Tata Workers Union Diamond Jubilee Commemorative Magazine*, 1982.

The SA8000 rationale

With a history of pioneering practices in employee welfare, what new vistas lie before Tata Steel in continuously improving the quality of life of its stakeholders as it journeys onwards to a global frontier? Searching for best practices and structural approaches, it was clear that "the challenging SA8000 standard provides an opportunity both for improving and demonstrating our commitment to best practices in the manufacture and supply of goods we sell and procure" (*Desire to Excel* 2004). And, thus, the initial groundwork toward certification such as the SA Policy, Management Review System, and awareness drive was laid in 2003–04 by the corporate Business Excellence function. The company's Steel Works in Jamshedpur attained certification and recertification in 2005 and 2007 respectively, and is one of the largest certified entities worldwide.

Key themes in implementation

The metaphor for SA8000 management system implementation in Tata Steel Works is similar to creating a ripple with enlightened partners, employees, vendors, suppliers, and non-governmental organizations, among others, *to generate a wider social impact through stewardship*. Progress on this cross-functional initiative involving key roles from the industrial relations, procurement, safety, and occupational health departments, among others, is tracked through various indices: external audits of suppliers and medical check-ups of employees and supply-chain workforce, to cite just a few examples. Representation of management, union, and departments across the company on the Management Review Committee have resulted in enhanced compliance through self-auditing and the creation of systems toward enhancing employee and supply-chain well-being.

Contracting and supply-chain compliance

The company initiated third-party audits in 2005–06 on SA8000 clauses for its principal vendors and suppliers. Coverage of over 100 major vendors has resulted in audit for 75% of the contract workers engaged through them at the Steel Works. A Vendor Assessment© form for service providers to Tata Steel, developed by procurement to check vendor, contractor, or subcontractor data for mandatory legal clearances, also includes a checklist for system review for SA8000 to be completed by them to enroll with Tata Steel.

Active engagement with contract labor and contractors has shown marked improvement in overall awareness on statutory requirements such as minimum wage, provident fund and employee state insurance benefits access, and working hours-related compliance on the part of vendors. In 2006–07 Tata Steel established and institutionalized a system for annual check-ups for contracted workers engaged in hazardous areas and over 52,000 employees have been covered in annual health check-ups. Attention was given to ensuring that those found unfit are not discriminated against but given medical aid and rehabilitated.

Extending skill development training at the company's Employees Training Centre has resulted in raising employability and productivity of contract laborers in trades such as mechanical and electrical fitting, gas cutting, and welding.

Measurement protocols

Third-party surveillance audits, internal audits, and second-party audits yielded substantial data in the initial years. As the system matured, a need was felt to replace the pen-and-paper check sheets with an audit tool that was consistent, uniform, and delivered actionable information about the vendor being audited. The Tata Steel SA8000 Vendor Assessment Protocol© was especially formulated for this purpose and since 2005 has served as the yardstick for compliance measurement on different SA8000 aspects. A comparative rating of vendor capability *vis-à-vis* SA8000 is generated automatically depending on their scores across the nine clauses. Corrective and preventive actions are then instituted by the vendor and verified by the auditors within a specific time-frame. Improvements have been seen in documentation and record keeping of statutory and basic provisions such as age verification, wages, and attendance register. Some vendors have also instituted internal policies on disciplinary practices and contracting which were not in place previously.

Employee facilities and services enhancement

Corrective and preventive actions based on six-monthly surveillance audits demonstrated progressively higher levels of compliance and improvement and strengthening of practices in the following areas:

- **Safety and occupational health.** Initial audit feedback focused on improvements such as safe work permits; critical task observation; severity reporting; streamlining accident data, reporting and investigation resolution time; and communication and counseling on health issues
- **Monitoring of work environment.** To achieve greater consistency in internal audit reporting, the Vendor Assessment Protocol© tool was modified to cover relevant points in the departmental assessment context. Providing a common platform and controlling for auditor subjectivity, the protocol captures data from personal interviews, documents, and site visits by trained personnel in designated departmental teams. Results are generated as numeric data and also graphically, and reviewed at various levels. In the upcoming annual planning cycle, efforts are under way to integrate internal audits and PDCA as part of departmental daily management

SA8000 as a complementary approach

No child labor

Tata Steel employs no child labor. The company's recruitment process requires furnishing appropriate proof of age for employment. The SA8000 clause on child labor guides communication to vendors and stakeholders that employment only of persons aged 18 and above is a precondition to partnering with Tata Steel, and that, in the event of discovery of a violation by vendors within or outside the company premises, liabilities for the education of the child until completion of high school will accrue to the defaulting party. To further consolidate efforts in this direction, in 2007 a process was created at the Rotary Foundation-affiliated Labor Training Center for age verification of contract labor, which lists the kinds of documentation required as age proof and includes provisions for medical examination.

SA8000 and human rights training

In ensuring that requirements of SA8000 and company policies are understood and implemented, classes are conducted at the in-house technical institute, with special modules geared toward new hires. In 2008, in addition to ongoing departmental sessions, nine training sessions were conducted for lateral hires, trade apprentices, and associate company recruits. Over 1,150 employees have been trained between 2004 and 2008, with the program scoring high participant satisfaction rating.

Equal opportunity

To further strengthen Tata Steel's equal opportunity employer practices, resulting from surveillance audits feedback, the role of the company's Ethics Counselor was broadened to serve as Ombudsperson on all SA8000 aspects; a Women Empowerment Cell representing women from company rank and file was constituted; and programs to raise awareness on legal aspects were extended beyond employees to cover women contract labor.

Going forward

The road to sustainable enterprise, negotiated across differing markets and regions with varying priorities, is seemingly moving away from the linear progression of individual bottom lines and moving toward drawing value from their interlinkages. Tata Steel seeks to generate both internal and external value for its stakeholders through focused awareness, voluntary self-review of workplace policies and procedures in reducing potential risk, and enhancing engagement and well-being in keeping with its founding values. Building synergy between shop-floor quality systems and the intangible domain of social workplace aspects is well served through the standardized approach offered by SA8000.

As a recent Center for International Private Enterprise (CIPE) and Social Accountability International (SAI) case study concluded, significant gains have been visualized in the areas of contract work and supply chain social compliance:

> Tata Steel has long been India's front-runner in good corporate citizenship, making the concerns of workers and of the community an integral part of its business operations. Given its history, size, and reputation, Tata Steel has significant potential to demonstrate the beneficial influence of adopting SA8000 in India and beyond. Improvements to its vendor management system, as well as contract workers' safety, health, and training prompted by implementation of SA8000, offer examples and guidance for other companies seeking effective approaches to meeting workplace standards (Kaufman 2009: 34).

Conclusion

With globalization, workplace and supply-chain issues are gaining importance from a corporate governance and social responsibility perspective. Ensuring fair and decent work standards at various stages of production is an unstated expectation of business in the competitive marketplace. For a business spread out across geographies, workplace standards are equally relevant for its highly skilled workforce, and also across its subsidiaries or outsourced operations which might be engaging unskilled or unorganized labor. For example, a culturally diverse multinational may need to create or revise internal policies on equal opportunity and disciplinary practices to bring about uniformity. At the same time, as the corporate and principal employer, it might need to establish procedures to monitor and provide assurance on issues such as child and forced labor, trafficking, health and safety, wages, and work hours to check for regional and national variances in the enforcement of labor laws. Frameworks offering system-wide review, compliance, and verification, irrespective of a company's location, size, or stage of growth, can help in identifying and addressing risks, at the very least. For the aspiration-driven enterprise, such frameworks can further support continual improvement and benchmarking critical to the attainment of long-term sustainability and "differentiating" business leadership.

References

Desire to Excel (2004) "What is SA8000?", *Desire to Excel* internal newsletter, February 2004.

Kaufman, Eileen Kohl (2009) 'The Case of Tata Steel: Including Contract Workers as India's Integral Business Stakeholders," in CIPE (Center for International Private Enterprise) and SAI (Social Accountability International), *From Words to Action: A Business Case for Implementing Workplace Standards. Experiences from Key Emerging Markets* (Washington, DC/New York: CIPE/SAI; www.cipe.org/publications/papers/pdf/SAI.pdf, accessed April 20, 2009): 24-34.

Lala, R.M. (1981) *The Creation of Wealth* (Mumbai: IBH).

3

OTTO and SA8000

A pilot project in the lingerie-buying department

Johannes Merck
Otto Group, Germany

History: OTTO's social management system and the role of SA8000

Fashion is the core product line of OTTO, the German multichannel retailer, which was established in Hamburg in 1949 as "Otto Versand." Since then, OTTO has developed into an international business and furthermore into a globally active trading and services group, the Otto Group. Since the 1990s, a large proportion of the textiles offered in the OTTO range have been manufactured in Asia. Toward the end of the last century it became increasingly apparent that suppliers' compliance with social working standards, despite quite strict legislation, was being inadequately monitored and ensured by the state. As a result, OTTO developed its Code of Conduct in 1996, which is oriented toward the relevant guidelines of the International Labour Organization (ILO). Since 1997 it has been an official component of the Supplier Framework Contracts. In addition to this, the Otto Group, with its flagship OTTO, expanded its own social management system during the course of the following years and has been heavily involved in multi-stakeholder initiatives and industry associations.

As a result, the company played a part in the multi-stakeholder process of Social Accountability International with the development of the SA8000 standard, which was initiated in 1997. At OTTO's suggestion, an industry solution was developed from the end of the 1990s in the Foreign Trade Association of the German Retail Trade (AVE), in which the member companies agreed in 2001 to require suppliers in all key import markets to maintain a minimum set of standards and to train them for this purpose. This AVE sector model was the first solution in the world where an entire industry agreed to specific social standards below which competition based on best price would no longer take place. Since 2004, the Otto Group has been involved in the Business Social Compliance Initiative (BSCI) developed under the auspices of the European Foreign Trade Association (FTA), which represents a further development of the AVE programme at a European level. (Lorenz Berzau provides more information on this in Chapter 7.) The BSCI aims for best practice in line with the SA8000 standard and suppliers should initially achieve the BSCI standard on a compulsory basis and then develop further toward achieving the SA8000 standard. The Otto Group assisted with the development of the BSCI standard and as a result is following a development-policy approach which is intended to improve working conditions in partnership with the suppliers. To achieve this, the supplier pays for the audit and for implementing the necessary measures, and the company pays for the qualification measures.

As part of its Market Development Programme, which the Otto Group has been running since 2003 in all relevant markets, suppliers are qualified through subject-related workshops and training courses and factory visits. They are also supported with implementing the requirements of the Corrective Action Plans from the audits. Between 2003 and 2006 alone, the Otto Group invested around €9 million in implementing this qualification program. Despite this, the guarantee that all violations can be prevented as a result of these checks and training sessions cannot of course be given, as experience has shown. For that reason, the Otto Group is putting everything into promoting the social competence of its suppliers in various ways—whether it be through appointing social officers in the import offices of the buying markets, who, for instance, run pre-scans (advance audits) for potential new suppliers; through posting to Shanghai a corporate responsibility (CR) representative for Asia who will drive forward the issue there at a political level; or through pilot projects to improve subcontractor monitoring.

The SA8000 project of the 49ers

Buying Area 49, which is responsible at OTTO for the underwear and nightwear range, has its products made in Asia, among other regions. However, one special aspect of its production process is that it works with producers of goods under license from other companies: the Buying Area also orders branded textiles from its own suppliers. If the Code of Conduct were to be infringed by these suppliers and this infringement made public, this would no longer simply reflect on OTTO; it would also—unjustifiably—reflect on the brand of the licensor. In this regard, OTTO therefore has a dual responsibility: to ensure socially acceptable production together with the supplier, and responsibility *vis-à-vis* the licensor. Due to this unique situation, Buying Area 49 decided, in cooperation with the Corporate Responsibility Department, to initiate accelerated implementation of the BSCI process across all buying markets and to commit suppliers to the SA8000 standard in the case of risk markets and risk lines. This project too was based on the premise of not just making demands but also providing support.

The BSCI auditing process was to be accelerated with all suppliers in the markets of Hong Kong, China, Mauritius, Thailand, Vietnam, Turkey, Macao, India, and Pakistan. Supported by corresponding qualification measures, they were to show within six months that they had passed the BSCI audit with a "good" result. In addition to this, the SA8000 standard was to be used as a tool in India and Pakistan to ensure licensed products were being manufactured in a socially responsible way (usually this applies to the finishing of fabrics made from cotton and polyester). This is because suppliers, particularly in India and Pakistan, frequently pass on work to subcontractors, which means the supply chain quickly ceases to be transparent. For this reason, Buying Area 49 decided to implement the SA8000 standard because it requires a management system that integrates the sub-suppliers, subcontractors, and home workers.

A key factor for success was that the project was top-management responsibility right from the start and the buyers agreed on clear procedural guidelines. Responsibilities were well defined, all employees mobilized, and all departments integrated (see Fig. 3.1): the buyers and buying managers in Buying Area 49; the Corporate Responsibility Department (VV-CR) with its representatives at Head Office in Hamburg and the Asia representative in Shanghai; the social officers and employees in the market offices; and the consultancy Systain, a wholly owned subsidiary of the Otto Group, which, among other things, specializes in carrying out qualification measures with suppliers.

FIGURE 3.1 Communication between all parties concerned

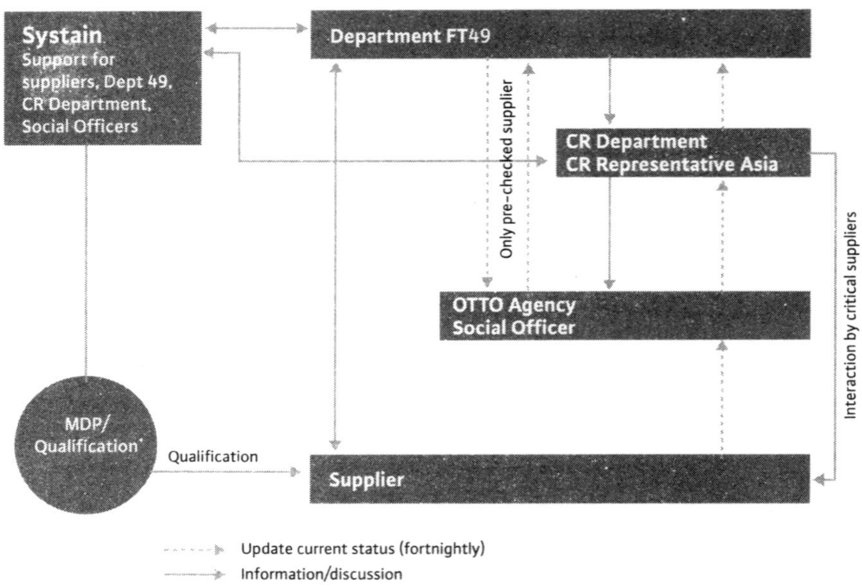

The timescale that was set was ambitious. At the end of February 2007, the Buying Area informed the various offices and their social officers about its social requirements as part of the pilot project. In March 2007, Sibylle Duncker, CR Senior Consultant at Head Office in Hamburg, and Morten Severon, Senior Manager of Planning and Allocation, Buying Area 49, went to Hong Kong and Shanghai to prepare for the project launch planned for April 2007. The suppliers were informed that this migration to SA8000 could be beneficial to long-term business relationships and that the order volumes were to be increased in the case of a consistently good price–performance ratio. Maren Wunschick, Quality Coordinator, Buying Area 49, says:

> The Pakistani suppliers were surprisingly open-minded about the SA8000 standard. There were also no widespread reservations in India, either. This was due to the fact that the advantages and opportunities of this step were clear to see: as a result of the introduction of the internationally recognized best-practice standard, it promised recognition and orders from other customers, too.

In the summer of 2007, employees from Systain and the CR Representative Asia, Maren Boehm, traveled through the markets and prepared the suppliers and production sites for the requirements of the SA8000 standard. Implementation was driven forward according to market and the importance of the licensed products. The buying trips that took place afterwards also had the aim of taking a close look at the initial successes and assessing the genuineness of suppliers' efforts. The aim: by mid-October 2007, the audit was to be passed with a "good" result as part of the BSCI in the markets of Hong Kong, China, Mauritius, Thailand, Vietnam, Turkey, and Macao. By the spring of 2008, a total of seven suppliers in Pakistan and India were to be approved for SA8000 certification.

Financing was governed in the following way, in accordance with our partnership approach: the supplier paid for the introduction of the SA8000 standard and therefore bore the twin costs of compliance and certification; from its Market Development Programme budget, OTTO paid the costs for intensive coaching by the consultancy Systain and, if applicable, would consider accepting higher prices on a case-by-case basis. A special situation existed in Pakistan regarding the coaching costs because the Pakistani government had decided to promote the implementation of the SA8000 standard more strongly in its own country and to support manufacturers in implementing it. Two OTTO suppliers have made use of the Pakistani government's offer.

Results and evaluation

The project was able to achieve its ambitious goal in the summer of 2008. All suppliers achieved the desired level and an additional three suppliers were added to the previous seven in India and Pakistan. Of these ten active suppliers, eight were SA8000-certified and two were undergoing the certification process. One of the certified suppliers succeeded in making the jump directly from a "critical" audit result to the SA8000 standard while the three additional newly added suppliers have made the jump from "a standing start," so to speak.

On the whole, all sides considered the progress of the project to be positive. The suppliers knew what opportunities lay for them in migrating—the SA8000 standard is internationally recognized and customers therefore do not need to insist on their own audit—and set deadlines themselves. But suppliers in other Asian markets as well, which "only" had to achieve a "good" BSCI audit result, were resolute in implementing this improvement and achieved a good BSCI audit result within the scheduled time requirements.

Positive feedback was received from the suppliers in India and Pakistan. They reported that their productivity had actually improved and that employees were happier after implementing the SA8000 standard, as both health and living standards had improved. However, suppliers also reported challenges posed by the SA8000 standard. Paying living wages as well as high certification costs generally meant higher production costs. Furthermore, the sophisticated SA8000 management system has to combat regional unpredictabilities. For example, some of the employees who had migrated to the region are interested in earning as much money as possible in the shortest possible time. Primarily they are not interested in welfare benefits or regulated working hours; rather, they search for an employer for which they can do as much overtime as possible. During harvest time and local festivities, they go home for several months at a time. This puts compliance with legally prescribed maximum working-hour regulations to the test, time and again.

The Buying Area that initiated the pilot project had, on the one hand, to incorporate increased organizational effort and financial outlay into its already streamlined processes and its scope of action. On the other hand, the greater security achieved made (and is making) a positive difference and is contributing greatly towards limiting the area's risk exposure. In addition, the improved conditions in the factories are making the job of supervision by the market offices easier. However, the feared price increases have also become a reality, although these could theoretically be due to different causes and cannot necessarily be attributable to the introduction of the SA8000 standard. Currency fluctuations, for instance, may also have been a factor for the price rise. Nevertheless, the difference is noticeable: since the migration to SA8000, purchase prices have in some cases risen by 10–12% from the suppliers involved in India and Pakistan. Moreover, during the implementation phase this led to longer delivery times. In the markets where a good BSCI audit result became mandatory within six months, the delivery times with some suppliers also rose due to social requirements; the purchase prices rose by around 5%.

That said, the overriding conclusion gained from this pilot project for all parties involved can be summarized by a very positive mood overall: "It works!" and "It works when we pull together!" The CR Representative Asia, Maren Boehm, summarizes:

> In this project, we have again learned just how important it is to work in partnership with the suppliers. As we deal with each other on equal terms and have developed mutual understanding for the respective difficulties and challenges, we have also succeeded in providing moral support and in successfully realizing the project in such a short time together.

The project has also contributed toward a further improvement in cooperation between buying and the market offices in terms of social compliance. CR Senior Consultant Sibylle Duncker underlines this from her perspective: "It makes it clear once again what opportunities unfold when each party involved in the production, buying, and procurement processes performs and implements its specific responsibility. Such a complex process cannot work without this degree of ownership."

Outlook

Striving toward the SA8000 standard in the social management system of the Otto Group, including OTTO, will also be a priority goal in the future. Overall, around 10% of all active suppliers are currently SA8000-certified in the Otto Group Social Programme. The ten suppliers of Buying Area 49 have made a decisive contribution towards this quota. Buying Area 49 will adhere to the aim of familiarizing new license producers in India and Pakistan with the SA8000 standard in the future. The market offices have been correspondingly informed that if a longer-term business relationship becomes apparent, the SA8000 standard will in principle be obligatory. Buying Area 49 is also aware of its responsibility regarding the future expansion of purchasing volumes from these suppliers and will bear this very much in mind alongside the many other influencing factors when placing orders.

The Otto Group social management system gives buyers the support necessary for this task. The stringent system relies on the responsibility of all parties involved and sets out clear aims. It is regularly subject to a management review which always allows room to identify new ways of doing things and to try out new approaches. For instance, the Otto Group took part in a Global Reporting Initiative (GRI) pilot project called "Transparency in the Supply Chain" where it supported suppliers in producing their own sustainability report in accordance with GRI guidelines. The project was successfully concluded in the fall of 2008, with all three of the participating Otto Group suppliers producing a report. More important than the report itself is the process that was initiated as a result by the suppliers who concentrated in-depth on the GRI criteria and in doing so defined the principle of corporate responsibility for themselves and their companies. The planned publication of the report created a new form of engagement in dealing with the topic.

Another foray by the Otto Group in the search for new ways of doing things is the "A Future Through Education" project. In March 2008, in partnership with the human rights organization Terre des Hommes, it launched a development policy project to combat child labor in India. The project has two regional foci: the capital New Delhi and the northern Indian state of Bihar, from where the majority of child labor is recruited to work in the major conurbations. Working with project partners from the region, under the leadership of Terre des Hommes and with the financial support of the Otto Group, children, youths, and their parents are offered various opportunities targeted at making a school education for children possible, thereby laying the basis for vocational training and enabling them to lead self-determined lives later on.

4

Gucci and corporate social responsibility

Franco Furnò and Stefania Orselli
Gucci, Italy

Gucci. The very name conjures up images of elegance, glamour, desirability, and decadence. Since the opening of its first store in 1921, Gucci has been known for products of outstanding quality and unmatched style. Luminaries ranging from Audrey Hepburn, Sophia Loren, and Madonna to Peter Sellers, George Clooney, and Lenny Kravitz have all sought Gucci's modern yet timeless sensibility.

While Gucci is immediately associated with the world of luxury and celebrity, fewer people know about the company's extensive commitment to social responsibility—a commitment that extends into the heart of Gucci's operations. Like many other successful businesses, Gucci has contributed generously to a wide range of charitable causes. The company's philanthropy was perhaps most widely displayed in the celebrations it hosted in New York to commemorate the opening of the world's largest Gucci store in early 2008. Gucci held a star-studded gala at the United Nations, raising millions for UNICEF and Raising Malawi's efforts to relieve the suffering of families in Africa devastated by the HIV/AIDS pandemic.

But, of course, corporate giving is only a minor component of real social responsibility. Gucci has long recognized that its commitments to social justice must be reflected in the way the company earns its money—not simply in how it spends it. At the same time, social responsibility has become an essential priority for Gucci's customers. In the modern luxury goods marketplace, excellence in craftsmanship, materials, and design must be coupled with ethical and responsible production.

Gucci strongly believes in creating sustainable value across its operations: combining commercial performance and financial discipline with respect for people, society, and the environment. It is not only possible to support social progress and responsibility in pursuit of outstanding business results—it is essential. In other words, Gucci strives to bring a new model of luxury to life.

To that end, Gucci—in close collaboration with both trade unions and key suppliers—has sought and received SA8000 certification from Social Accountability International (SAI). This far-reaching certification program analyzes and monitors every aspect of Gucci's Italian supply chain in jewelry and leather goods to ensure respect for human rights, fair treatment of workers, and safe working environments at every point within the Gucci system. In this chapter, we will look closely at the substantive efforts Gucci has made to receive SA8000 certification and deliver sustainable value across its supply chains for jewelry and leather goods.

The Gucci System

Gucci has long recognized the interaction and interdependence of all of its stakeholders in its commercial and industrial operations. Gucci's leadership thinks of its network of customers, employees, retail partners, suppliers, sub-suppliers, trade unions, local communities, and investors as a single system—wherein each component complements and supports the others. Each part of the Gucci System makes a vital contribution to the system's overall success—and the concerns and needs of each member must be met in order for the system as a whole to thrive.

Thinking of its business as a system helps Gucci deliver sustainable value to all of its stakeholders. The concept of the Gucci System forms the basis of the company's management policies and its rules of conduct for its employees and suppliers. Even before seeking SA8000 certification,

Gucci promoted sustainable value across the company through the adoption and application of nine key principles (see Fig. 4.1).

With these principles at the heart of its business, it was a straightforward step for Gucci to pursue official certification of its operations. The company had already developed a clear set of values intended to define and develop its business culture. While such principles inform actions across the company, it can be difficult to measure progress against such ideals in practice. SA8000 certification gave the company the structural framework necessary to assess, revise, and improve its operations to meet high objective standards.

FIGURE 4.1 Gucci's nine key principles

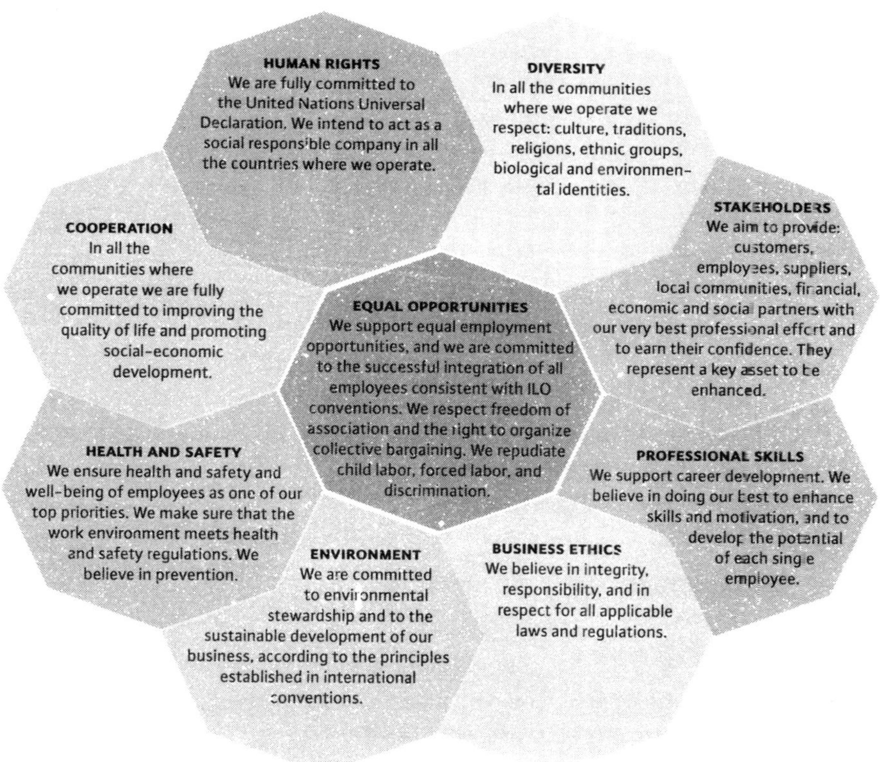

SA8000

Corporate social responsibility (CSR) is a rapidly growing field—with any number of potential standards, certifications, and organizations promoting improvements. When seeking to formalize the commitments outlined in the values of the Gucci System, Gucci reviewed a wide range of potential certification paths. For Gucci, the standard had to meet several criteria for adoption.

First, the standard needed to be internationally recognized and consistent. The credibility of the company's efforts in CSR would be judged by the certification standard Gucci chose—so it had to be one that business leaders, trade unions, and informed stakeholders would recognize and respect. Next, the standard needed to focus on the issues of collaboration, respect, and social justice that matter so greatly to Gucci. Third, it had to be rigorous. There is little point in pursuing a goal unless it entails real effort. Finally, it had to be realistic and practical.

After careful review, SA8000 was the clear choice. With its focus on working practices and labor standards—crucial issues in the luxury goods industry—SA8000 provided a rigorous and structured framework for optimizing operations across the Gucci System.

SAI developed the SA8000 standard in 2001, drawing on the principles of the International Labour Organization, the Universal Declaration of Human Rights and the UN Convention on the Rights of the Child. The SA8000 standard comprises nine key elements:

1. **Child labor.** No workers under the age of 15; minimum lowered to 14 for countries operating under the ILO Convention 138 developing-country exception; remediation of any child found to be working

2. **Forced labor.** No forced labor, including prison or debt bondage labor; no lodging of deposits or identity papers by employers or outside recruiters

3. **Health and safety.** Provide a safe and healthy work environment; take steps to prevent injuries; regular health and safety worker training; system to detect threats to health and safety; access to bathrooms and potable water

4. **Freedom of association and right to collective bargaining.** Respect the right to form and join trade unions and bargain col-

lectively; where law prohibits these freedoms, facilitate parallel means of association and bargaining

5. **Discrimination.** No discrimination based on race, caste, origin, religion, disability, gender, sexual orientation, union or political affiliation, or age; no sexual harassment
6. **Discipline.** No corporal punishment, mental or physical coercion, or verbal abuse
7. **Working hours.** Comply with the applicable law but, in any event, no more than 48 hours per week with at least one day off for every seven-day period; voluntary overtime paid at a premium rate and not to exceed 12 hours per week on a regular basis; overtime may be mandatory if part of a collective bargaining agreement
8. **Compensation.** Wages paid for a standard work-week must meet the legal and industry standards and be sufficient to meet the basic need of workers and their families; no disciplinary deductions
9. **Management systems.** Facilities seeking to gain and maintain certification must go beyond simple compliance to integrate the standard into their management systems and practices

Each of these principles is consistent with the values and ethics of the Gucci System. The final principle insists on ongoing integration of these standards—making it an ideal tool for optimizing Gucci's supply chain.

A collaborative approach

Gucci's decision to pursue SA8000 certification was prompted by the company's desire to have a clear, measurable standard for social responsibility across its supply chain. The goal for Gucci was to develop a practical framework for implementing the company's values and for acting on its ideals.

An undertaking of such breadth and scope demanded a collaborative approach between Gucci, its employees, its suppliers, trade unions, and the local communities in which Gucci operates. For Gucci to implement and be certified for meeting the SA8000, all of these parties would have to work together, openly and cooperatively, to realize shared goals. To that end, Gucci and the Joint Trade Union Delegation for the Industrial and Retail Areas signed a Memorandum of Trade Union Agreement to Promote Social Responsibility on June 10, 2004.

Within the business, Gucci needed to take a balanced approach to adopting and implementing the SA8000 standards across the supply chain. If Gucci's management simply insisted on new ways of working and new policies and procedures, without consulting employees, suppliers, and trade unions, the entire initiative would be doomed to failure. In fact, even with a positive goal in mind, top-down, management-driven reforms would contradict the spirit of SA8000.

To ensure collaboration and contribution from people across the business, Gucci has established the Joint Committee on Social Responsibility. The committee's remit is very clear: to make sure that practices at every point on the leather goods and jewelry supply chains comply with SA8000 standards. To do this, the Joint Committee seeks input, ideas, and recommendations from employees, suppliers, and stakeholders across the production network. The Joint Committee reviews existing practices and analyzes other areas of the business and assesses recommendations for change. Where activities or policies don't make the grade, it is up to the Joint Committee to find practical ways of meeting the certification requirements. At the same time, the Joint Committee holds responsibility for promoting awareness of and attention to social responsibility across the Gucci System.

The membership of the Joint Committee is what truly helps the group succeed. The Joint Committee on Social Responsibility is made up of an even mix of people appointed by Gucci's senior management and by people selected by the trade unions representing the employees of Gucci and its suppliers. This balanced membership means that a wide range of opinions, ideas, and suggestions are considered by the Joint Committee. It means that people with different perspectives on the business share common goals and bring their distinctive expertise to the group's task.

Experts on workshop conditions work alongside financial counselors and communications professionals developing workable solutions to overcome complex challenges. The diverse membership of the Joint Committee helps to make sure that the process of developing and adopting new procedures is as transparent as possible. The success of Gucci's social responsibility initiatives depends on people at every level of the organization knowing what is happening and why. Having such a wide-ranging group working as a team encourages openness, clarity, and frank dialogue.

Gucci has also sought an independent body to audit the company's supply chain for SA8000 certification. While the Joint Committee identifies areas for change, it is essential to have independent verification for an internationally recognized standard such as SA8000. Accordingly, Gucci contacted Bureau Veritas Italia (BVI), one of the world's most highly esteemed certifying bodies, to provide independent assessments of the company's supply chain and the actions of the Joint Committee.

The work of the Joint Committee does not end with SA8000 certification, however. On the contrary, improving the social performance of the Gucci System is an ongoing task. The Joint Committee continually seeks ways to further improve operations across the Gucci System—not only to meet or exceed SA8000 standards, but also to reduce the company's environmental impact. Every year, the Joint Committee sets new targets for social performance, which are verified in the annual management review.

Making it work: implementing SA8000 standards at Gucci

The main role of the Joint Committee is to implement policies and procedures that meet SA8000 standards at every point across the Gucci System. To approach this enormous task, the committee has identified four functional areas for action. The Human Resources function addresses performance indicators for working conditions and employee relations. Supply Chain Management measures the performance of Gucci's suppliers and sub-suppliers in complying with SA8000 requirements. The Audit function keeps track of ongoing inspections and assessments, while the Management System monitors the overall progress of the SA8000 Social Responsibility Management System. Within each functional area, Gucci has identified a set of performance indicators that it monitors closely. The Joint Committee regularly reviews progress in each area and takes appropriate action to ensure that targets are met and goals are achieved. This tracking system is known as the SA8000 Social Responsibility Management System Dashboard (see Fig. 4.2).

FIGURE 4.2 SA8000 Social Responsibility Management System Dashboard

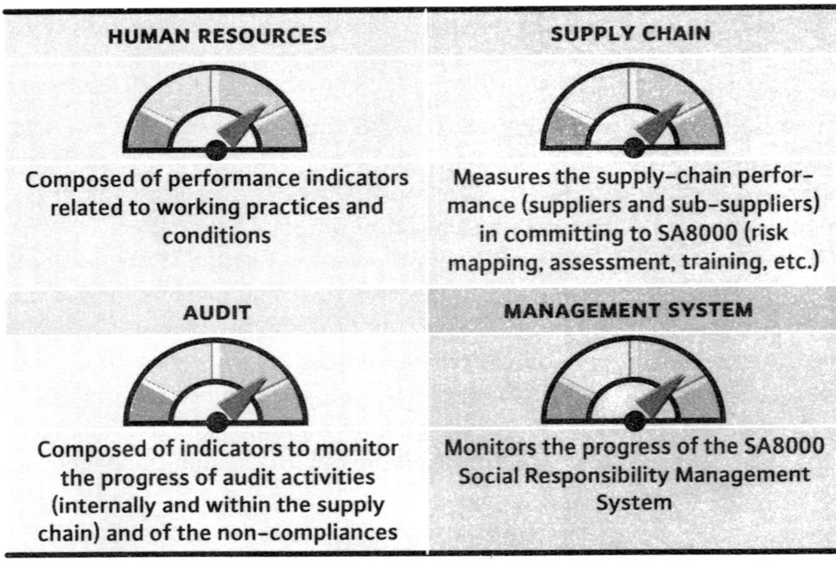

Human resources

The SA8000 standard is, in nearly every respect, about protecting the rights, interests, and well-being of people. Accordingly, the effective management of human resources (HR) within the Gucci System is crucial to the achievement of the company's goal of SA8000 certification.

Gucci has always prized the contributions of its people. Support for career development, enhancing skills, encouraging strong motivation, and helping people realize their individual potential are central to Gucci's values and are deeply embedded within the company's culture. In keeping with these values, and in compliance with the SA8000 standards, Gucci has adopted several measures that support and demonstrate its respect for people.

Child labor

The first measure is the company's refusal to use child labor anywhere in its supply chain. Gucci monitors its own operations, its suppliers and, in turn, their suppliers—to make sure that child labor is not part of the production process. The company has also committed to support the remediation and education of any children discovered working at any point on its supply chain, in the very unlikely event that an underage person is employed by the company or its suppliers.

Reporting non-compliance

Every employee has both the right and the responsibility to report activity or procedures that are inconsistent with Gucci's values and, more specifically, with SA8000 standards. The company encourages people to report any concerns openly and honestly—and it even provides means of anonymous reporting so that concerns are expressed and heard. Employees can report issues to the company, to SAI, or to the certification authority, BVI. Gucci will not take any measures against employees reporting non-compliance with SA8000 standards. The Joint Committee is responsible for verifying the facts of any allegation and taking corrective action wherever necessary.

Mobbing

Bullying or mobbing of any employee for any reason is wholly unacceptable. Gucci promotes mutual respect, tolerance, and cooperation between all of its people, and it takes issues of physical or psychological intimidation very seriously. The company has developed policies for staff to report (anonymously if necessary) any incidents of mobbing, bullying, or harassment and for the company to take remedial action swiftly.

These policies help Gucci address several provisions of SA8000. To achieve certification, however, careful review of HR policies and procedures is essential. To that end, Gucci has tracked a series of demographic data and key performance indicators.

Personnel Map

Gucci maintains a Personnel Map that provides a clear overview of the diversity and demographics of the company's workforce. Gucci tracks these data so that it can promote a culture of respect, tolerance, and cooperation across the business. The Personnel Map helps Gucci monitor several vital pieces of information, and that information prompts important questions about the business:

- The comparative number—on a percentage basis—of senior management, middle management, and non-managerial employees. Is the ccmpany too top-heavy? Are there enough people providing leadership? Do people have a clear point of reference to address issues?
- The number of women working in the company and the number of women working in managerial or leadership roles. Are men and women fairly represented across the business? Are men and women given equal opportunities for advancement?
- The percentage of Italian and non-Italian employees, managers, and senior leaders. Is the company recruiting a broad spectrum of people? Does the company provide equal opportunities for advancement, regardless of background?
- Average age of employees, managers, and senior executives. Do people have fair opportunities for advancement, regardless of their age?
- Advancement and development of people over time. Is the company helping people develop? Are there clear opportunities for people to develop their skills, advance in their roles, or to take on new challenges?

Another element of the Personnel Map helps Gucci classify how staff are compensated for the work they do—ensuring consistent and fair standards based on skills and experience. This comprehensive approach also includes provisions for regular evaluations so that employees can move progress between classification bands.

Performance indicators

While the criteria tracked in the Personnel Map help Gucci understand the profile of its workforce and encourage fair opportunities for people of any age, gender, or background, the performance indicators required for SA8000 certification are even more detailed. In order to receive certification, Gucci needs to make sure it achieves compliance in a large number of areas, including but not limited to:

- On-the-job injuries
- Wage hours

- Strike hours
- Personnel turnover
- Terminations
- Ratio of fixed-term to unfixed-term contracts
- Number of employees joining trade unions
- Trade union disputes with negative outcomes
- Absenteeism
- Disciplinary actions

Tracking this information not only helps Gucci qualify for the SA8000 standard, but, even more importantly, the data allow the company to examine its operations very closely and identify ways of improving performance—for the sake of its people and its performance overall.

Supply-chain management

The implementation of SA8000 standards within Gucci's own facilities and operations is only one part of the certification process. To receive complete certification, Gucci has worked with its suppliers and sub-suppliers to apply the SA8000 standards at every point of its supply chains for jewelry and leather goods.

To do this, Gucci has worked in close partnership with its suppliers to improve their processes and to help them, in turn, support improvements among their own suppliers. Gucci has considered its suppliers and their employees as partners in the overall effort of improving the social responsibility of the entire Gucci System. Together with suppliers and sub-suppliers, Gucci has used the SA8000 framework to

- Establish a shared language of social responsibility. Common terms and concepts help drive consistency across the supply chain
- Communicate targets and share tools with suppliers and sub-suppliers. By using similar measures and procedures, all of the parties involved in the supply chain make progress
- Support suppliers in making positive changes in their own operations and helping them work, in turn, with sub-suppliers. Collaboration between parties lies at the heart of the Gucci System

- Propose new actions to improve social performance and ensure correct implementation. Continuous improvement is vital to long-term success

In order to help its suppliers understand and adopt the SA8000 standards, Gucci has produced a series of communications tools, information kits, and explanatory materials that make the company's targets and objectives clear. In July 2006, Gucci held a special workshop for its suppliers so that they could learn about and explore the implications of SA8000 compliance together. Additionally, Gucci has carried out a series of intensive training seminars to help its own employees and key personnel within its suppliers learn more about labor law, occupational health and safety, maintenance procedures, and outstanding management.

Using a sophisticated risk-assessment tool, Gucci has helped its suppliers identify potential areas of non-compliance or even risk within their operations. Suppliers, in turn, apply the same risk-assessment methodology with their sub-suppliers. Just as Gucci secures commitment from its direct suppliers to respect and implement the SA8000 standards, the company's suppliers come to the same stringent agreement with sub-suppliers. This supply-chain mapping program has allowed Gucci and its suppliers to prioritize areas for improvement and take action in the areas that will make the greatest difference.

Auditing

Inspection and assessment are crucial components of the SA8000 certification process. Independent, unbiased, and rigorous review of practices within Gucci and its suppliers help to make sure that intentions for excellence are being realized and that words are being followed up with action.

Gucci and its suppliers have made major progress in this area. With the support of BVI, the company has been able to address issues at several points across the Gucci System to bring the entire network up to expectations.

The auditing process has also helped make good relations between Gucci and its suppliers even better. By committing to the standards of transparency demanded by the auditing process, Gucci and its suppliers have a much better understanding of each other's needs, concerns, methods, and requirements. By following a consistent approach to improving social accountability, the entire Gucci System is becoming more consistent and more efficient as well.

Gucci personnel regularly visit supplier premises—and suppliers visit their sub-suppliers—to make sure that everything is operating properly and in accordance with expectations. Gucci now has a much clearer understanding of the network of companies supporting its own direct suppliers, and agreements are in place to maintain exacting standards whenever a new supplier is considered for inclusion in the Gucci System.

Management system

The final indicator of progress on the dashboard is the overall management system for SA8000 implementation. Gucci's most senior management have made realization of the SA8000 standard a top business priority for the company—and have made the company's commitment to excellence absolutely clear.

Senior managers within the company regularly assess the progress and activity of the Joint Committee and provide guidance and resources to make sure the committee can improve operations across the Gucci System. Every year, the company's most senior leaders review actions, consider recommendations, and commit to targets for continued improvement. Following the plan–do–check–act framework outlined in Figure 4.3, the company's management cooperates fully in the pursuit of SA8000 standards.

Social responsibility has become a driver of performance across the Gucci System. Together, employees, managers, suppliers, sub-suppliers, trade unions, and investors collaborate in a continuous cycle to make sure that the Gucci System puts the company's values into clear, measurable, and visible action.

Figure 4.3 Plan-do-check-act framework

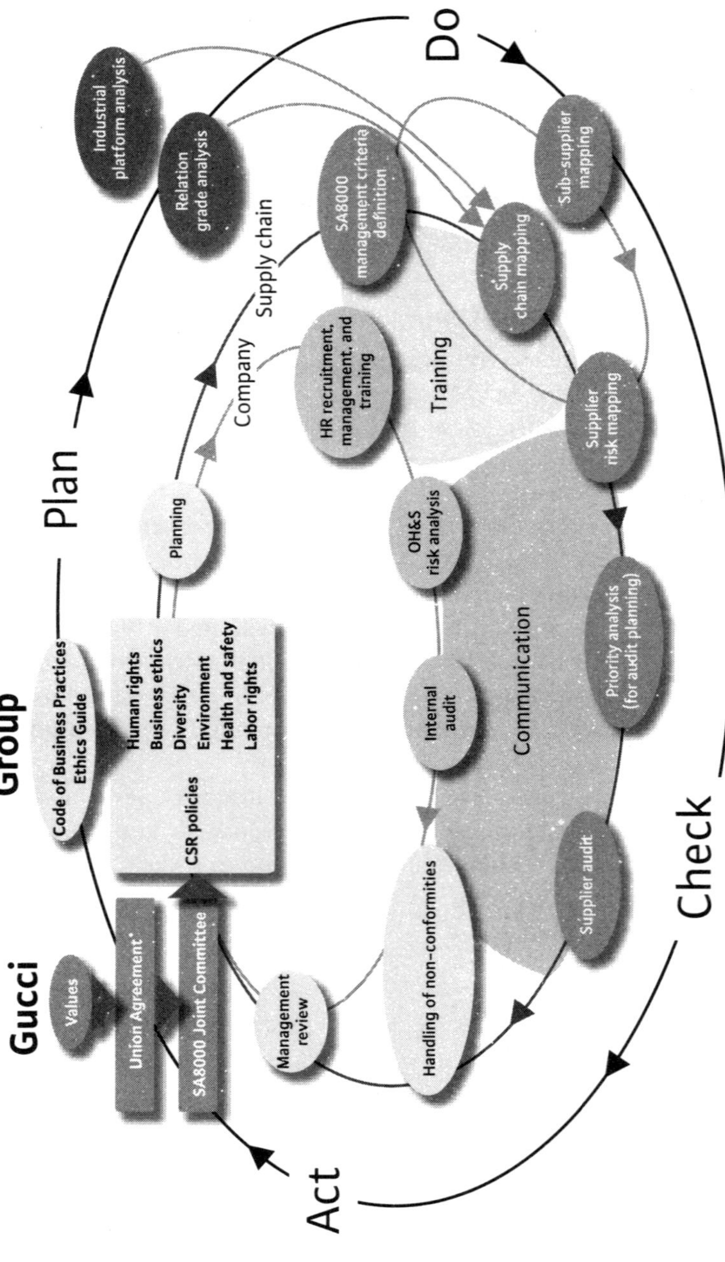

5

Gap Inc.'s journey toward corporate social responsibility

Dan Henkle
Gap Inc., United States

Every company with a supply chain, especially one that extends overseas, faces the challenge of ensuring not only that its suppliers produce goods that meet rigorous quality standards but also that these goods are made in factories that meet internationally recognized workplace standards. To hold suppliers accountable for a safe, healthy, and humane workplace, Gap Inc. has evolved over the past decade from a corporate social responsibility (CSR) model that was based primarily on a team of internal auditors to a more collaborative partnership model in which factory owners and managers are expected to take more responsibility or "ownership" for working conditions. This chapter shares some key aspects of this journey toward ongoing social compliance. It attempts to demystify what a company can and should do to improve working conditions in its contract supply chain, and discusses in detail one resource—the Social Accountability 8000 (SA8000) workplace standard—that provides a way to empower factory management and help companies manage the demand for socially responsible sourcing.

Social responsibility in the supply chain

Although the global supply chains of apparel and footwear companies were the first to come under public scrutiny, the spotlight of stakeholder attention continues to expand. It is no longer a question of *if* a company will be held accountable for workplace standards at factories it owns or with which it contracts, but *when*.

At Gap Inc., we have found that the more we work to improve labor conditions in supplier factories, the further we have to go. Unfortunately, there is no simple answer and no "silver bullet." But we believe that, by improving our ability to identify violations, embedding labor standards directly into our business practices, and partnering effectively with our stakeholders to address systemic problems, we can help drive lasting change both in our approved contract factories and across the garment industry as a whole. We also believe that the lessons we have learned are applicable to other industries that source products through global supply chains.

In 1996, we wrote our own Code of Vendor Conduct based on internationally accepted labor standards and built an internal compliance program complete with our own compliance monitors. In doing so, we sought to apply consistent standards and ensure uniform performance across our supply base. Our goal was to be accepted as objective and credible by a growing constellation of stakeholders—from non-governmental organizations (NGOs) and socially responsible investors to trade unions and governmental bodies. However, experience has taught us that simply building our own internal "policing" staff is not the most effective path to better working conditions. Unless factory managers assume ownership for compliance in their facilities, we find ourselves in a never-ending cat-and-mouse game of trying to uncover non-compliance with our standards. Moreover, we have learned that credibility with stakeholders is not won by internal systems alone, no matter how extensive or well intentioned.

The good news is that companies that are just beginning to grapple with human rights in their supply chains do not need to reinvent the wheel. They can take advantage of existing and evolving expertise in standards development and third-party monitoring. They can learn from the experience of Gap Inc. and other companies that are leveraging established resources such as the SA8000 standard. They have the opportunity to utilize auditing systems that encompass multiple industries rather than just one. They can also establish credibility with their stakeholders more easily by adopting a standard that is the product of multi-stakeholder participation and by having their suppliers monitored by auditors who have no business interest in the outcome of the audit.

Most importantly, companies taking the first steps to address social responsibility issues in their supply chains can make supplier ownership a key requirement in the auditing process. No company can or should look over the shoulders of its suppliers every day. Factory owners and managers must be committed to workplace standards of fair and humane treatment and, more critically, need to implement management systems to ensure these standards are put into operation. Saying the right words is not enough. Even the right actions are not enough. Policies, procedures, and clearly defined roles, responsibilities, and administrative structures are vital building blocks in bringing about sustainable compliance.

Gap Inc.'s journey to partnership

The way in which we manage problems at Gap Inc. stems in part from the kind of company that we are. As a $14.5 billion international specialty apparel retailer[1] that offers new products every season, we make decisions rapidly and have learned to adjust our approach or change course based on market demand. Historically, when a problem has arisen, our approach has been to recognize it, fix it, and move on.

In 1995, Gap Inc. faced allegations of serious labor rights abuses at Mandarin International factory, a third-party garment supplier in El Salvador, as well as a national campaign by the National Labor Committee to spotlight these abuses. We chose to tackle the problem both on the ground level in Central America and at the corporate level. Gap Inc. collaborated with three NGOs—Business for Social Responsibility (BSR), the Center for Reflection, Education, and Action (CREA), and the Interfaith Center on Corporate Responsibility (ICCR)—to form an Independent Monitoring Working Group (IMWG). The IMWG engaged the Grupo de Monitoreo Independiente de El Salvador (GIMES), a group of representatives from Salvadoran civil society who sought to help workers in the maquila sector. The effort marked the beginning of the first independent monitoring

1 Gap Inc.'s revenue in 2008 was $14.5 billion.

program in El Salvador and in the apparel industry globally. In addition, we took a step back as a company and reflected on the effectiveness of our compliance program, which had been built originally on the sourcing principles and guidelines we had adopted in 1992.

We ultimately responded with the development of a new, more operational Code of Vendor Conduct in 1996 based on internationally accepted labor standards, as well as the creation of a separate internal Global Compliance department to approve and monitor factories in our supply chain. We quickly built up one of the largest compliance programs in the apparel industry. Today we employ approximately 80 people around the world who are dedicated to addressing social and environmental issues and improving the lives of garment workers in our supply chain. From the beginning, we sought to hire people who were from the country in which they would work, and who would understand the language and culture of workers and managers. Our current team members come from incredibly diverse backgrounds; many of them worked previously in the NGO, trade union, or government sectors and see their work as a way to help improve the lives of their fellow citizens.

Today, our internal auditors are skilled at spotting observable health and safety issues, such as blocked aisles and crowded floors, inadequately stocked first aid kits, or the absence of mesh-cutting gloves in fabric-cutting sections. Most of these types of issue are relatively easy to fix and do not require much additional time or training. We have realized, however, that our auditors are less effective with some of the more challenging issues—for example, those associated with labor and wage requirements, such as excessive overtime, "double books," and other subterfuges to hide actual hours worked; discrimination in the promotion of workers; and interference with workers' rights to organize and bargain collectively. Our monitors have often found themselves identifying problems and requiring the factory to resolve them, only to uncover the same (or related) issues on the next visit.

In its first five years, our compliance program was predominantly a reactive model of monitoring. We came in, told the factory what was wrong, and the factory fixed what we told them to fix. The factory waited for us, as their customer, to tell them what we wanted. Our compliance officers often made multiple visits to a factory to monitor improvements on the same problem. Unfortunately, this is not an efficient or effective way of implementing social workplace standards. Moreover, despite some concrete advances in workplace conditions attributable, in part, to our compliance efforts, skepticism remains on the part of many labor and human rights experts about internal company monitoring programs.

Over time, we have come to realize that it is not enough to try to improve workplace conditions one discrete corrective action at a time. To bring about lasting improvements in working conditions, our suppliers must have a fundamental commitment to respect human rights and need to develop the management capacity necessary to incorporate it into the way they conduct business. Many of our suppliers are multinational companies in their own right. As such, we are looking at ways to encourage them to assume responsibility for conditions in the factories that they own and operate.

When we speak of embedding labor standards directly into business practices, we now also understand that this means addressing not only the practices of our suppliers, but our own practices as well. We are currently looking at how our own production decisions—rush orders or last-minute changes in style or quantity, for example—may contribute to the very problems of excessive overtime or mistreatment of line workers that our compliance staff then has have to correct. We are also working to refine our integrated supplier scorecard that evaluates our suppliers on their compliance performance—along with performance on cost, speed, quality, and innovation.

In addition, we have come to realize that our monitoring staff will be most effective in the long term if they utilize their expertise to partner with factories and help them build up factory management systems that support ongoing compliance. By reaching out and partnering with multiple stakeholders on assessment, training, and capacity-building programs, we are able to make the most of our internal resources and leverage our business relationships with suppliers.

We also believe that we can help to effect broader industry change by working through multi-stakeholder initiatives such as the Ethical Trading Initiative (ETI), Social Accountability International (SAI), the Business Leaders Initiative on Human Rights (BLIHR), and the Global Reporting Initiative (GRI), as well as focused efforts such as the Joint Initiative on Corporate Accountability and Workers' Rights in Turkey, the Multi-Fiber Arrangement (MFA) Forum, and training programs in Guatemala and other Central American countries.

Leveraging existing resources: SA8000

As Gap Inc. has become more involved in multi-stakeholder initiatives, we have had the opportunity to examine external resources that may help advance ownership of social responsibility in our own supplier base and in the industry. A resource of much interest to us is SAI: in particular, the SA8000 standard and its model of sustainable improvement.

Why SA8000?

Several noteworthy aspects of SA8000 create the foundation for a more sustainable solution to compliance:

- SA8000 is a global, cross-industry standard, with requirements that are applicable to industries producing all types of goods and services, from apparel to electronics to agriculture
- SA8000 creates a level playing field for facilities regardless of their country location and maximizes the credibility of facility performance in one industry by linking it to a multi-industry standard
- SA8000 goes beyond the requirements of local law by harmonizing with International Labour Organization (ILO) conventions, the pre-eminent source of principles and goals in the human rights field
- SA8000 is an auditable standard based on the International Organization for Standardization (ISO) model. Companies familiar with ISO 9001 and ISO 14001 will find SA8000 understandable and feel relatively comfortable with its requirements to institute management systems that support continuous improvement. Moreover, its concept of certifying that a process is in place to address a particular set of problems is not alien to business leaders; it is common in other aspects of business operations, such as financial management and quality assurance
- SA8000 has performance provisions with a key focus on interviewing workers. Worker interviews are an important component of performance credibility, since it is workers' complaints that often drive more worker–management interaction and, ultimately, improvements in factory conditions. At least 30% of an

SA8000 auditor's on-site time in the factory is reserved for these interviews

What does SA8000 ask suppliers to do?

SA8000 asks each supplier facility to comply with applicable national and local laws and regulations and meet requirements in nine areas: child labor, forced labor, health and safety, freedom of association and the right to collective bargaining, discrimination, disciplinary practices, working hours, remuneration, and management systems. The language of the SA8000 standard and its Guidance Document helps factory managers understand in operational terms what they should strive to attain.

A key element that distinguishes SA8000 from most corporate codes of conduct is the requirement for management systems that form an infrastructure of policies, procedures, roles, designated responsibilities, training, and communication to support social accountability—in other words, systems that institutionalize commitment and ownership and will therefore survive even when personnel changes. Simply put, SA8000 says to factory management, "Anyone can talk the talk. You must also show us that you can walk the walk." As part of SA8000 certification, when factory management takes ownership of compliance, it commits the factory to a basic plan–do–check–act model of continual improvement.

The SA8000 management system includes procedures that verify and sustain implementation of the other eight SA8000 performance elements mentioned above. The facility should have records that document past performance and give auditors and companies reasonable assurance that similar (or improved) performance will continue in the future. Unlike systems that focus on production processes, the SA8000 management system is designed to protect workers' basic rights, improve working conditions, and enhance worker–management communication. It addresses five basic elements—policy and planning, implementation, performance review and evaluation, corrective action, and communication—that help the factory treat its workers in a planned and less arbitrary way. In asking a facility to take ownership of compliance, SA8000 also places responsibility on the facility to ensure that any additional facilities that directly or indirectly supply or subcontract with it also meet the SA8000 standard.

Who decides if suppliers are meeting SA8000?

In 2005 and 2006, Gap Inc. terminated business with a total of 85 factories for non-compliance with its Code of Vendor Conduct, and in 2006 we rejected 18% of the new factories inspected by our own auditors. Nonetheless, critics of internal compliance programs contend that, even if a company has a sound set of labor standards, a company's credibility as an objective auditor may be compromised by the need to initiate and/or maintain a business relationship with key suppliers.

SA8000 helps to avoid this controversy. Neither the buyer nor any self-appointed auditing organization is authorized to certify a facility—only organizations accredited by SAI can do so. To achieve accreditation, an organization must undergo a process similar to licensing in which SAI evaluates the organization's capacity to audit a workplace for compliance with SA8000.

The accreditation evaluation includes an office review, witness audits to observe how auditors conduct an SA8000 audit, and periodic surveillance audits. After an auditing organization has been accredited, it remains subject to ongoing review and oversight by SAI.

This accredited third-party audit system gives companies greater confidence that standards will be applied consistently across suppliers. It also creates the opportunity for a more productive relationship between a buyer and its suppliers by reducing the need for a perpetual policing system and strengthening the opportunity for partnership.

What does a supplier have to do to attain SA8000 certification?

Preparing for and achieving certification is a step-by-step process that develops a facility's capacity to meet the requirements of SA8000. Even before the audit, the initial assessment and audit preparation process provide opportunities for a factory manager to look constructively at policies, procedures, and operational systems and implement changes appropriate to his or her particular situation. In the case of SA8000 certification, the journey is as important as the destination.

The time required for certification varies according to the starting point and capabilities of the individual facility. It can take as long as three or four years for a factory to become SA8000-certified. However, several Gap Inc.-approved garment manufacturers that chose to pursue SA8000 certification were able to earn it in less time. For example, four Gap Inc.-

approved suppliers in China achieved it in five months or less, and two in Sri Lanka qualified in two-and-a-half months and seven months, respectively. By the end of 2007, more than 75 Gap Inc.-approved factories had been certified to the SA8000 standard.

An investment worth making

Apparel manufacturers invest in machinery and production management systems—from needle detectors to automated embroidery machines to computerized pattern-making programs—to improve product quality, manufacturing efficiency, and productivity. The cost of these investments is measured against operational benefits and, ultimately, the benefit of having a reputation for quality products. There is no doubt that social accountability in the workplace, like the quality of finished garments, comes at a price. A supplier who embarks on a process to take ownership of compliance and SA8000 certification assumes additional costs: internal management and personnel time—both audit-related and for staffing the ongoing management systems; external consultation; training service; and making required improvements in response to findings from the assessment audit, third-party certification audit, and regular surveillance audits. Is this investment worth it?

Benefits to suppliers

SAI's research and findings point to a range of benefits for suppliers that include increased worker morale and productivity, decreased turnover and absenteeism, increased efficiency, and improved product quality. As a consequence of these benefits, a supplier is better positioned to build long-term relationships with particular buyers and is thus in a more competitive position to build its customer base.

The benefits of SA8000 for a supplier's apparel manufacturing operations can perhaps be best illustrated by the experience of one factory, Apparel Avenue, the first factory in Thailand to receive SA8000 certification. Building on previous ISO certifications in 1998 and 1999, the factory found the SA8000 process relatively easy to implement in 2000. The factory's quality assurance manager observed that employees familiar with the implementation of quality standards "perceive change in a positive way because every time that change takes place, they believe that this new standard will improve their working environment again" (Rohitratana 2001: 83).

By organizing an internal SA8000 working group under the leadership of the human resources manager, the factory was able to deal creatively with the thorny issue of overtime. Under Thai law at that time, a workweek could not exceed 48 hours on a regular basis, with a maximum of two hours of overtime per week. Working with the production engineer, the factory team was able to redesign work stations and work processes so that, after a three-month implementation period, overtime was reduced to the required level with a simultaneous increase in worker productivity. SA8000 and the changes it necessitated led to a mutually beneficial solution for managers and workers. The work environment was improved, the company reduced its overtime costs, and the workers made the same amount of money working fewer hours.

Other suppliers have reported similar benefits. For example, Pre[illegible] Durai, an SA8000-certified apparel factory in Tirapur, India, experienced significant improvements in output, product quality, reduced employee turnover and absenteeism, and a 52% decrease in overtime in just one year after it implemented better working conditions to comply with SA8000 standards.

Benefits to buyers

From the perspective of companies such as Gap Inc., a supplier base of certified factories provides a distinct advantage for both workplace conditions and production needs. The company has more confidence that products will meet quality specifications and delivery timelines. It has greater assurance that goods will not be subcontracted to facilities that do not meet its production or human rights standards. There is also less risk that its reputation will be harmed by human rights abuses in a factory where its goods are being produced—a harm that is costly to bear and not easy to repair.

At Gap Inc., we view SA8000 as a premier set of global labor standards toward which we hope our garment manufacturers will aspire. As we noted above, more than 75 of our current suppliers have already received SA8000 certification. As a member of SAI's Corporate Involvement Program, we recently completed a gap analysis of our Code of Vendor Conduct relative to the SA8000 standard and published a revised code in 2008 that is in closer alignment. In addition, the majority of our auditing team completed the SA8000 auditor course in 2005.

Toward the goal of sustainable change

In Gap Inc.'s 2005–2006 Social Responsibility Report, John Ruggie, the Special Representative of the UN Secretary-General on Business and Human Rights observed that "companies have made our world a global village. Now they must help keep it livable. Because if it can't be made to work for all, in the end it will work for none."

At Gap Inc., we have been encouraged to see how ethical sourcing has evolved from the writing of codes of conduct to the development of internal compliance systems, and now to the concept of sustainable improvement in working conditions with an emphasis on shared responsibility and ownership between brands and their suppliers. While we know that there is much more work to be done, we hope that the incremental improvements already taking place in many apparel factories are the beginning of real progress toward the goal of safe, healthy, and humane working conditions around the world.

We know that there are no easy answers. Yet we believe that real, tangible, sustainable change is possible if brands, retailers, suppliers, governments, trade unions, and civil society come together and work collectively to develop solutions that address the underlying causes of poor working conditions. The growing number of external resources available to help companies, such as SA8000 certification, is an encouraging sign. It is our hope that companies will increasingly recognize that responsible sourcing practices are, in fact, in their best interest and will seek out the resources, partners, and practical tools they need to ensure that these practices are implemented effectively throughout their supply chains.

Reference

Rohitratana, K. (2001) "How to effectively implement SA8000 in Thailand," in S.K.M. Ho and M. Donnelly (eds.), *Proceedings of the 6th International Conference on ISO9000 and TQM* (Ayr, Scotland: Paisley Business School).

6

Chiquita and corporate responsibility

The fruits of our experience

George Jaksch
Chiquita International S.G., Belgium

The evolution of corporate social responsibility at Chiquita

Chiquita has dedicated considerable effort and resources to implementing a coherent corporate responsibility program. While much still remains to be done, this is a good time—ten years after we first used the term "corporate responsibility"[1]—to draw conclusions from this experience.

Chiquita Brands International was formerly called the United Fruit Company. Under that name the company developed—indeed, virtually invented—the business of the international banana trade some 100 years ago. It rapidly expanded, coming to own huge tracts of land in the tropical regions of Latin America, establishing settlements, farms, ports, and

1 Corporate responsibility (CR) and corporate social responsibility (CSR) are one and the same thing: a voluntary program to systematically establish high standards of legal, ethical, social, and environmental conduct in a company.

railway systems in the thinly settled and unhealthy lowlands, and as a consequence exercising great influence in the region. Much has been written about abusive practices of the company: for example, in its relations with the governments of the region. But the company also contributed to the control of malaria, and provided schools, health systems, and year-round employment to many thousands of local inhabitants and migrants. Looking back, one should not overlook the historical context: a period when "civilization" had a very different meaning.

Chiquita is still a banana farmer of substance, employing some 17,000 men and women in banana production. But the era of dominance ended years ago. Today, two-thirds of Chiquita's banana shipments originate on the farms of local growers, with whom the company often has long-standing contractual relationships. Despite many and continuous efforts to diversify, the banana trade is still the company's primary source of income, and the oval blue Chiquita label has come to symbolize a well-known brand in many countries.

The evolution of the corporate responsibility concept at Chiquita has gone through four phases:

First phase: Rainforest Alliance

The notions of sustainability and corporate responsibility began their career in this company, when the Rainforest Alliance, an environmental non-governmental organization (NGO) based in the United States, urged banana producers to implement its new standard for sustainable banana production. This organization had developed social and environmental criteria for banana production, based on its experience of the certification of tropical forestry. At a meeting in 1991, the Rainforest Alliance presented a new vision of banana farming to skeptical industry executives: farms that passed an annual audit by representatives of the Rainforest Alliance and the other members of the Sustainable Agriculture Network would qualify for the Rainforest Alliance certification. Auditors were to have access to all workplaces, documents, and employees. This was a huge departure from the historic industry model of self-contained farms where outsiders were kept at arm's length.

David McLaughlin, then the general manager of Chiquita's Costa Rican operations (now with WWF), had the vision and courage not to reject this notion out of hand, but instead to evaluate the Rainforest Alliance concept. Initially, tests were conducted on two farms in Costa Rica, which achieved certification in 1994. As a result of this positive experience, the company publicly committed to Rainforest Alliance Certification, and in 2000 completed the certification of all owned farms in Latin America. Some $20 million were invested in improvements on these farms to bring them into compliance with the Rainforest Alliance standards—a considerable sum at a time of low profitability. Since then, the company has focused on ensuring that local banana suppliers also meet the same standard and obtain the certification. Changes in the contracts with suppliers, technical assistance, and in many cases a financial incentive resulted in the adoption of the Rainforest Alliance system by hundreds of banana growers. By 2005, over 90% of these producers had earned the certification. This permitted the company to ensure that supplies to key markets in Northern Europe would come from certified farms. Since late 2005, Chiquita bananas sold in Scandinavia, Germany, Switzerland, Austria, and the Benelux companies carry the "Rainforest Alliance Certified" seal next to the Chiquita label.

The advertising campaign that announced this change introduced millions of European consumers for the first time to the concept of sustainability certification and the Rainforest Alliance. It is estimated that some 15% of the international trade in bananas now originates from Rainforest Alliance-certified farms. Chiquita remains the market leader in the valuable European banana market, not least because the Rainforest Alliance certification responds to the increasing awareness of social and environmental issues among retailers and consumers.

What motivated the company to embark on this far-reaching commitment? Several factors were at work. The pressure from campaigning NGOs was a contributing factor, but the decisive impulse came from within: managers were willing to forge a radical departure from traditional ways, even when the business benefits were far from evident.

The experience of the work with the Rainforest Alliance created the foundation for the following phases, especially:

- The exposure of all employees to the ideas of social and environmental responsibility, as a result of regular training and the experience of implementation
- The successful adoption of an external standard and external verification

Second phase: Code of Conduct and SA8000

In 1998, Chiquita's then president Steve Warshaw called on his team to develop a concept of "corporate responsibility," which would enable the company to ensure and demonstrate that it acted responsibly and as a good citizen wherever it operated. The CEO took a strong personal interest in the work that followed.

A corporate responsibility steering committee was formed to develop the framework and advise the CEO and his senior management team. This committee still meets today.

The first task was the development of "core values"—a set of principles that would provide the foundation for all subsequent activities. A very detailed process of consultation led to the Core Values that today are on display in all workplaces, and are printed on the back of Chiquita business cards. They are organized under four headings: Integrity, Respect, Opportunity, and Responsibility (Box 6.1). Employees contributed close to one thousand suggestions and comments during the development of these core values.

The next step was the development of a new code of conduct, to replace an earlier version which had not been widely communicated. The new Chiquita Code of Conduct, published in 2000, included guidance on the meaning of ethical conduct, reference to legal and ethical requirements, and a significant additional chapter on human rights in the workplace. After considerable discussion, the steering committee decided to adopt the SA8000 social accountability standard as the basis for this chapter: the standard is quoted in full with only minor adaptations. SA8000 offered important features:

- A standard based on national laws, international human rights norms, and the conventions of the International Labour Organization (ILO)
- Developed by experts including trade union leaders
- Independent audits and certification
- Management system requirements for consistent implementation over time

Subsequently, internal and external auditors conducted gap analyses to evaluate the degree of compliance, and external experts from trade unions and NGOs were invited to participate in the annual assessments

Box 6.1 Chiquita's Core Values

Integrity

- We live by our Core Values
- We communicate in an open, honest, and straightforward manner
- We conduct business ethically and lawfully

Respect

- We treat people fairly and respectfully
- We recognize the importance of family in the lives of our employees
- We value and benefit from individual and cultural differences
- We foster individual expression, open dialogue, and a sense of belonging

Opportunity

- We believe the continuous growth and development of our employees is key to our success
- We encourage teamwork
- We recognize employees for their contributions to the company's success

Responsibility

- We take pride in our work, in our products, and in satisfying our customers
- We act responsibly in the communities and environments in which we live and work
- We are accountable for the careful use of all resources entrusted to us and for providing appropriate returns to our shareholders

by internal auditors. The SA8000 certification of Chiquita's owned banana farms was completed in 2004 in five countries, the first such certifications in Latin American agriculture.

The publication of the new Code of Conduct was followed by corporate responsibility training of all employees following the cascade principle (starting at the top). In some years over 20,000 employees participated in such training sessions.

In 1999, Jeff Zalla became Chiquita's first Corporate Responsibility Officer, in recognition of his decisive leadership. Chiquita began to publish corporate responsibility (CR) reports in 2001. The frank presentation of the results of Rainforest Alliance and SA8000 assessments in the first CR Report was met with praise: SustainAbility and the United Nations Environment Programme (UNEP) rated Chiquita's report the best in the food industry, commenting on its "courageous account of weaknesses."

Third phase: framework agreement with trade unions

These developments were observed with skepticism by trade unions and NGOs. A high proportion of Chiquita's employees in banana production are members of trade unions, and in most countries working conditions, wages, and benefits are reflected in formal collective bargaining agreements with local trade unions. In 2001 Chiquita entered into an International Framework Agreement (IFA) with the International Union of Food Workers (IUF) and COLSIBA, the coordinating body of Latin American banana workers unions. The Director General of the ILO was witness to this agreement, the first IFA to be signed by a U.S. company, and the first in the banana industry.

This agreement, which applies to Chiquita's banana production activities in Latin America, commits the company to comply with the Core Conventions of the ILO. It also establishes a Joint Committee, which is to meet at least twice a year to review progress and address any problems that have not been resolved by local negotiations. The signatories agree that the trade unions will abstain from international campaigns, and that the company will not interfere with the exercise of workers' rights.

The Joint Committee has met regularly to this day. While discussions have not been without controversy and tensions, Chiquita's IFA has had an outstanding consequence: the number of strikes and stoppages has declined considerably, and the devastating confrontations of the past have largely been replaced by dialogue and negotiations. Furthermore, critical observers have applauded Chiquita for this innovative engagement.

Fourth phase: partnerships and cooperation

Chiquita's commitments to corporate responsibility have opened the door to collaboration with others, the breadth and depth of which is a new phenomenon. The sustained corporate responsibility effort has generated goodwill and trust, which is an essential precondition for any sustained relationship.

In Honduras, the government and local authorities collaborated with Chiquita in creating a new housing development for banana workers. As a result, over 1,500 workers have become homeowners—a far cry from the long-standing dependence of workers on housing provided by the company. This project won the 2004 Corporate Citizen of the Americas Award of the Organization of American States.

In Costa Rica, the Swiss retailer Migros and the German development corporation GTZ have partnered with Chiquita in the Nature and Community Project, which aims to conserve biodiversity by protecting forests, planting biological corridors, and involving local communities and institutions. This project has received several awards.

Chiquita's corporate responsibility work is neither finished nor always successful. Nevertheless, the years of effort have taught us some valuable lessons.

Corporate responsibility: lessons and conclusions

Looking through the admittedly imperfect but pragmatic lens of our accumulated knowledge, the following pages will focus on three questions which any company concerned with CR or CSR will need to consider:

1. A working definition of corporate responsibility—what should it include?
2. What are the indispensable building blocks of a respectable CR effort?
3. Implementing CR—what are the important steps?

Corporate responsibility: a definition that works

Any newspaper reader will be aware of how difficult it appears to be for businesses to integrate ethical notions into the way they operate. A chasm seems too often to separate the fine words and good intentions from the reality of the business operations. What does it take to bridge this chasm? Part of the answer lies in the operational definition of corporate responsibility—four elements are indispensable:

The concept of duty

It needs to be abundantly clear throughout the organization that the company recognizes its duties as a responsible citizen. These duties involve:

- Compliance with laws. It is often said that CR goes beyond legal requirements. However, it needs to be understood that compliance with laws is by no means a self-evident axiom, and indeed wherever governments are weak or corrupt one can observe chronic failures of companies and citizens in general to comply with the law of the land
- Regard for ethical values and human rights that are universally accepted and applicable in every corner of the globe
- The principle of the company as a good and responsible citizen, with duties toward society and the environment

The principle of discipline

"Zero tolerance." These words and corresponding actions send an unmistakable message that:

- Every employee, business decision, and activity is expected to comply with the organization's ethical standards
- This rule will be vigorously communicated and enforced
- Any failure to comply will be subject to substantial penalties

The principle of dialogue and cooperation

This principle takes into account the fact that the company operates in a dynamic social context which is subject to constant change. The exchange of ideas and information with stakeholders and critics enables the company to make better choices, to recognize opportunities for improvement, and to act as a responsible citizen.

A clear definition of the geographical and organizational scope of the company's CR commitments

- Does it apply to all owned and controlled operations? Newly acquired companies, joint ventures, and partnerships with majority ownership, subsidiaries, and representatives? New product design and development, marketing, and communications?

- Does it include the upstream supply chain: suppliers of goods and services?
- Is it legitimate to exclude certain business units or parts of the supply chain from a company's CR activities? The author's perspective:
  - For a CR policy to be credible, one of the first areas of application should be those activities under the direct control of the company. Even when the company's owned operations may be thought to be well regulated and with little risk of CR failures, it should be remembered that the principle of leading by example is of great importance when changing a culture and encouraging participation
  - On the other hand, it is entirely acceptable for a company to progress the implementation of CR concepts in manageable stages, as long as this staged implementation shows steady progress

CR: the indispensable building blocks

Certain key features and components should be present in any respectable CR effort. The following questions will shed light on the reality:

1. Are the principles of respect for the law and ethical conduct securely and durably anchored in the organization?

Like so many energetically announced initiatives, so also may CR well disappear without a trace, leaving only a few dusty manuals and brochures for future researchers. How to enable this concept to survive the inevitable changes of management and priorities? If the goal is to make CR a core element of the organization's culture and even traditions for generations to come, then it will be essential to integrate CR into strategy, objectives and planning, organization and performance management, incentives, and rewards.

2. Is the implementation of the CR concept evaluated and measured in a systematic and credible manner?

Increasingly recognized external standards, which are periodically verified by external audits, are emerging as best practice. SA8000, a standard for labor rights, is an example of this mechanism: annual audits evaluate compliance with a precisely defined standard based on internationally established human rights as they apply to workplaces. Such systems offer significant advantages:

- **Discipline.** The result of independent and thorough assessments
- **Objectivity.** An efficient audit process executed by external auditors avoids the risks of undue influence and pressure which can affect the quality of internal audits
- **Knowledge.** Employees are required to know and understand the standard, and regular training must be documented
- **Continuous improvement.** Any deficiencies detected during the audit lead to a "corrective action" process which is evaluated during subsequent assessments

However, internal control processes are also essential. Employees must be able to report any violations or illegal conduct confidentially or even—if desired—anonymously. Regular internal audits, in connection with an effective corrective action process, are valuable instruments for implementation of corporate responsibility.

3. Dialogue and cooperation: what is done?

CR should include the active exchange of ideas with stakeholders, which enables the development of a societal perspective, and quite possibly the solution of problems as a result of this cooperation.

This dialogue also needs to extend to the representatives of employees and trade unions, in full compliance with the ILO Core Conventions. On the international stage these are often absent or incomplete. Framework agreements provide an instrument for constructive cooperation of multinational enterprises and the international trade union federations.

The possibilities of cooperation go well beyond the boundaries of a company's factories and farms. The great problems of our time, such as the AIDS epidemic in Africa, climate change, and the loss of biodiversity can only be effectively addressed with the active participation of business.

Implementing CR: the important steps

Corporate responsibility is—or certainly should be—more than a fashionable but ephemeral trend: it needs to be recognized as a profound change in the organization's culture. CR cannot be imposed on the organization, as might be the case with a new accounting system. CR only has a chance of success and survival if a strong consensus and new convictions are created and the people of the company can be persuaded to adopt and participate in the necessary changes.

Here are some guidelines:

1. Values are the foundation

The endless debate about the "business case" of CR should not distract us from the fact that CR is based on a foundation of ethical values. The formulation of these values is not a quick and easy exercise. Who should they apply to? To the company and its officers? Employees when they are acting on behalf of and within the company? Our recommendation is that they should explicitly apply to the company and its employees. While there are many variations on the theme of values, certain core concepts need to be present, such as integrity, respect, solidarity, and responsibility—these are evidently values that have a place in the conduct of employees and the company itself.

Another key question is who should participate and be responsible for the creation of the "core values." In some cases, the CEO or a small circle of senior managers has taken on this task, but however well intentioned, this "top-down" implementation of values is unlikely to enjoy much credibility. The outcome will have much greater support and durability if employees are invited to participate in this process in a spirit of commitment and openness. The ideal end result: the people of the company will refer to the company's "core values" as "*our* values."

2. Decisive influence of company leaders

As with any important project, the key role of the CEO as an initiator and leader of the CR process cannot be overstated. This is not about efficient project management: the CEO and his or her senior managers set an example and exercise a deep influence on the thinking and conduct of personnel. Ethical values need to be lived to be believed.

3. Building consensus

The ideas of corporate responsibility should be shared and supported by the company's people at work. To achieve this takes a systematic and sustained effort, focusing on understanding, conviction, and support:

- **Understanding** means that employees are aware of company's CR standards and the underlying reasoning. To cultivate and sustain this awareness in culturally and geographically dispersed organizations is a substantial and continuous challenge
- **Conviction** is the result of consistent implementation and authentic leadership
- **Support** is encouraged by involving employees and by giving them the opportunity to contribute and participate

It is to be expected and entirely understandable that a CR initiative may initially be viewed skeptically by employees, influential leaders, and trade unions. Management will do well to take early steps to convince the skeptics that this effort deserves and needs their support. The most effective method is to invite them to participate in the creative phase and subsequent implementation.

4. Training and awareness

Employees everywhere need to know the company's CR policy, but how is this lofty ambition to be realized? There is only one way: a systematic and well-planned campaign of education, beginning at the top of the organization, and spreading in cascade fashion to reach every workplace. This is achievable only with the visible leadership of the CEO and his or her team and the involvement of managers and supervisors throughout the organization. Their personal participation sends a clear message: "This is important."

But this formal process is only one—albeit indispensable—way to spread the knowledge. The entire portfolio of communication and motivation tools is available to provide continuity, inject new ideas, refresh commitment and belief, and avoid repetitive preaching. But one thing should not be forgotten: the immediate supervisor usually has the most influential voice.

5. External standards and assessments

Internal standards and audit processes can be quite fragile and short-lived. Our experience with the Rainforest Alliance and SA8000 standards has demonstrated the benefits of adopting and systematically implementing authoritative external standards.

6. Dialogue and cooperation

The respectful dialogue with external observers and critics, however difficult this may sometimes seem, can generate valuable understanding and in the best case may provide novel solutions to chronic unresolved problems. Engaging with critics can over time lead to strong support from these same NGOs and individuals.

7. Dealing with failure

In any large organization, mistakes will be made and human weaknesses will surface. The best CR policy will be challenged by occasional ethical failures and illegal conduct. Such situations are the truest test of the organization's commitment to high standards and transparency. The best policy consists not only of immediate and effective corrective action, but also of frank and open disclosure of any failures and subsequent action. The end result of this difficult but necessary process will be heightened trust and credibility, the priceless asset that is so hard to earn.

Corporate responsibility: an investment in the future

Like any corporate endeavor, CR needs to be addressed with care, good planning, and leadership. If well executed, it can become an integral and positive part of a company's culture, its brand, and its reputation. If neglected, it may also become a significant liability, a hollow promise. For those very reasons the tactics and strategy of implementation need to be carefully considered, and the necessary continuity and institutionalization provided for.

The adoption of high CR standards protects a company's reputation and business and is therefore part of a prudent risk-reduction strategy.

More than a defensive measure, it is also an instrument to demonstrate excellence, to attract good employees, and to gain and retain customers and consumers.

These are good business reasons for promoting corporate responsibility. But companies have responsibilities that go beyond financial and commercial success; they are citizens, and have the duties of citizens to contribute to a peaceful, just, and well-ordered society. Companies exercise influence among their employees and the communities where they operate, and as such are a factor shaping our society and the world our children and future generations will inhabit.

Corporate responsibility is good for business, and good for society.

7

Business Social Compliance Initiative

The development approach to SA8000 for commerce and manufacturers

Lorenz Berzau
Foreign Trade Association, Belgium

CSR in the supply chain: from individual solutions to more synergies

For more than a decade, companies have sought to understand the term "corporate social responsibility" (CSR) in general and how, in particular, companies could bring social responsibility into their global supply chain. In the early 1990s, companies had already begun to implement practical control mechanisms based on corporate codes of conduct and monitoring systems in order to meet the criticism of the media, campaigns, and other stakeholders. Companies have recognized the need to incorporate such monitoring processes into the structure of the company. The reasons for companies to position themselves as socially responsible can be quite varied—ranging from mere considerations of risk management to philanthropically oriented business management. As competitors commit themselves to make their supply chains more socially responsible, there is growing motivation for companies to start or join projects as well.

Now the focus is no longer on "whether" but on "how" and "with whom." As a rule, the monitoring systems of individual companies were based on the same or similar standards and often geared toward the same supplier companies—mostly in developing countries. As a consequence, some suppliers had to undergo up to 70 social audits in one single year. Since different customers had to comply with different criteria, in some companies three different check marks were made at the same place, one below the other, for hanging up fire extinguishers, in order to satisfy the respective social auditors. Moreover, all these audits, which often were only marginally different from each other, followed the same aim: the control of social standards. This and the example of the fire extinguishers show that it makes sense to align the different solutions. Streamlining standards and policies is effective not only for supplier companies but also for companies in the industrialized world.

Within this context, joint models were developed at the national and sectoral levels in order to unify standards and processes. In Germany, at the end of 2002, the AVE Sector Model Social Responsibility of the Foreign Trade Association of German Retail Trade (AVE) was launched. This initiative began as a public–private partnership project together with the German Technical Cooperation (GTZ). The GTZ is an international cooperation enterprise for sustainable development owned by the German Federal Government. This system was joined by eight German companies and in 2003 by ten Dutch companies.

The BSCI as a development-oriented approach toward SA8000

In 2003, the Foreign Trade Association (FTA) in Brussels, representing the interests of importing European retailers, initiated the Business Social Compliance Initiative (BSCI). With the BSCI, a joint European platform for consistent auditing and qualification of suppliers was created. Around 20 companies from Germany, France, the Netherlands, Switzerland, and Sweden, and also Canada, were involved in drafting the system and its numerous instruments—a Code of Conduct, Audit Questionnaire, Audit Report samples, Guidelines for Auditors, Manual for Suppliers, a database, etc. The tools of the AVE Sector Model were integrated in the development of the BSCI, and the AVE system was later completely transferred to the BSCI.

As in the AVE system, the founders of the BSCI did not want to reinvent the wheel. The drafters merged and consolidated the most important existing standards. SA8000 was seen as the leading and internationally recognized standard supported by stakeholders. The group developing the BSCI agreed to form a system with the aim of steadily developing suppliers toward the implementation of the SA8000 criteria and finally toward certification. This development approach is a key element in the BSCI, as it has been seen that it can take a long time until suppliers are able to meet the SA8000 criteria. Thus, SA8000 is considered best practice for the BSCI. Suppliers meeting the BSCI Code of Conduct criteria are encouraged to go further toward achieving full SA8000 certification.

After more than a year of development work, the training and auditing of suppliers under the BSCI system began in autumn 2004, and by the end of 2007 the number of BSCI members exceeded 100. Major retail companies, producers, and small importers from ten countries have joined the BSCI. As of mid 2008, the list of companies comprises not only the textiles retail sector but also producers of lighting, kitchenware, and toys. Since spring 2007 the BSCI model has also been implemented within the supply chain of the food sector.[1]

The BSCI's central decision-making body is the Members Assembly. The BSCI features six committees to address major decisions. There are working groups on the issues of system development, system implementation, communication, (agricultural) primary production, qualification and training, auditing, and member acquisition.

BSCI members are committed to integrate into the BSCI process two-thirds of their soft and hard goods suppliers (textiles, clothes, footwear, toys, sports goods) within 3½ years in predefined risk countries (mostly in Asia, Africa, and Latin America): that is, they must at least carry out auditing within these companies. This commitment is to enhance the credibility within and outside the BSCI.

BSCI's Supervisory Board controls the implementation of the commitment and, if need be, proposes to the Members Assembly the suspension of members.

1 For a list of members see www.bsci-eu.com.

In the first six months of its membership, a company takes all necessary measures to implement the BSCI system. It is crucial that the company informs all relevant managers within the company about BSCI membership and integrates the different departments into the process—especially the purchasing, quality management, and public relations departments. The more the company management pushes this process internally, the easier it is to integrate the BSCI system into the company's daily practice.

The training of buyers is of major importance to the BSCI, since here is the concrete interface between European trading (or importing) companies and suppliers. Stakeholders remind us that, among other things, purchasing practices are responsible for non-compliance with social standards. Since this is a valid discussion, purchasers are made aware of this topic and receive training. In addition to quality, price, and delivery dates, the social and environmental performance of a company plays an important role when it comes to purchasing decisions. However, one should also recognize that the risk of non-compliance with delivery dates, which leads to suppliers engaging subcontractors and increasing working hours, is mainly due to a lack of planning on the producer's side. But as often is the case, one-sided accusations do not yield a solution. Purchasers and suppliers alike have to be trained in CSR, and, if they cooperate as partners, solutions can be developed.

Transparency in the supply chain and training courses

Another important step for the implementation of the system is the creation of transparency in the supply chain. Companies must be transparent about where the imported products are produced. Often, the production sites are not known, especially when products are bought via importers. Depending on the size of the BSCI member, the development of transparency mechanisms can take quite a long time. For example, if a company knows about a producer in China, it then has to find out whether this producer has its products made or partly made by subcontractors. If yes, transparency will have to be fostered there, too. BSCI members provide their suppliers with the BSCI Code of Conduct and a self-assessment questionnaire so that they get a better picture of a supplier's company structure and social performance. Moreover, the supplier is introduced to the criteria of the BSCI and can check how it might be assessed in a social audit. This is already part of the preparation of the supplier for the auditing and qualification process.

Very often, the high degree of complexity of global supply chains is underestimated. For example, the existence of shirts with a label of a European company in a production site does not mean, that this European company is the owner of the production site. Nor does it mean that there is a direct business relationship between the production site and the European company. It is also possible that the latter does not even know about the production site. This is due to the increasing mobility of production.

The BSCI organizes workshops in supplier countries, inviting those suppliers who are still at the very beginning of the BSCI process to participate. During these workshops explanations are given on the BSCI's mission, procedures, and management tools. The instruments are distributed to the participants in the respective local language and in the course of the workshops there is dialogue and discussion. These training sessions are geared to the managers of the production sites, since the main focus is on improving and implementing management systems. Moreover, BSCI members offer such regular training courses on an individual basis, which can be done easily within the framework of other supplier training courses and informative meetings on other topics.

The importance of audits in a long-term process

In order to monitor the criteria of the BSCI Code of Conduct, social audits are an important part of the process. They are carried out by independent auditing companies. The auditing companies have to be accredited by Social Accountability International (SAI) and, since early 2008, this is now conducted by Social Accountability Accreditation Services (SAAS). The auditors have to take part in SA8000 training courses and to pass corresponding exams. The independence and the quality of the audits are of major importance to the BSCI. The accreditation process is crucial to the system's credibility. The audits are the basis for drafting correction plans that describe in detail which measures have to be taken within what period of time, in order to ensure compliance with the criteria of the Code of Conduct.

By the end of 2007 over 3,000 audits were carried out in more than 30 countries, most of them in China, India, Bangladesh, and Turkey. The results, which are regularly published by the BSCI in its annual reports, vary from country to country. However, they clearly show that implementation of the criteria is most difficult in the following areas: compensation, working hours, management systems, and occupational health and safety. The main problem is that the management systems at the production sites of developing countries with work-intensive manufacturing processes are, very often, poorly developed or non-existent. Often the management staff do not have sufficient basic economic and organizational knowledge, which quickly results in non-compliance with numerous criteria—especially in peak production times. For example, the company owners realize too late that they are not able to meet the production deadline and order extra hours which they will would not be able to pay. Moreover, they pass on part of their production to a subcontractor whose social performance they do not know. Since the subcontractor has not made sure that the employees have access to clean drinking water by installing a filter system many of them get sick, so in addition to excessive overtime the production is hampered by absences and an increasing number of accidents. This is a sad scenario for the workers on the one hand—and for the company owners as well. The example shows that often the management is just stretched and needs help.

The audit serves to identify all of the deficiencies in social performance, and correction plans are set up which lay out the measures and deadlines for improvement of performance. The audits—especially the initial ones—are announced so that the manufacturing company can prepare itself for the audit. This has met with some criticism since it offers the opportunity to cover potential problems just for the period of the audit. BSCI takes this into account by increasingly carrying out unannounced re-audits in order to monitor the implementation of the correction plans. Moreover, the auditor has to talk with the company management and documentation has to be examined. If the audit were unannounced, this would not be possible in many cases. However, audits also have their limits. For example, the identification of violations of the ban on discrimination has turned out to be difficult. It is also difficult to establish whether the workers' rights to freedom of association and to collective bargaining are implemented effectively. The auditors also know that some company owners try to deceive them. In some regions these techniques have been perfected; however, ultimately they are of no avail for the companies.

Nevertheless, audits are and will remain an important step toward the creation of transparency for the importing company and the production sites. In recent years, the practice of auditing has often met with criticism by stakeholders. Companies who have been struggling to improve the social standards in their supply chains have seen the weaknesses of audits. Therefore, the quality of the audits is paramount. For this reason, the BSCI exclusively works with SAAS-accredited auditing companies, and auditing training is another element to enhance audit quality. Since 2007, the BSCI has also started to have audits verified by SAAS in order to ensure adherence to the auditing guidelines. This approach is currently intensified to enhance quality control.

Training and qualification: a key to sustainable improvement

For a development-oriented approach more is needed than just audits; hence the significance of audits should neither be underestimated nor overestimated. The auditing results show in which areas production sites need support.

Therefore, the BSCI's strategic planning focuses on training projects which can address:

- Management systems
- Techniques aimed at reducing overtime work and increasing wages
- The establishment of a social dialogue in the companies

An intense follow-up after the implementation of corrective action plans by the suppliers is essential in order to improve social performance. But follow-ups alone are not always sufficient. Increasingly, the BSCI and its members involve suppliers in training projects.

In Turkey, 80 suppliers and subcontractors participated in a project supported by the European Commission and organized by the BSCI together with SAI and the Istanbul Association of Textiles Producers and Exporters (ITKIB). Within the framework of this three-stage project, which ran from August 2007 until summer 2008, local trainers acquainted the participants with, in particular, the subjects of management systems and social dialogue. Both are keys to a good social performance in other fields, too, such as wages and working hours.

In October and December 2007, the BSCI together with SAI carried out a two-stage training project for 40 suppliers in Vietnam, which was supported by the U.S. State Department. Here, too, the trainers looked into the actual local situation, and training content was based on audit reports.

In the future, it is planned to conduct more of these projects in addition to the annual workshops the BSCI organizes for suppliers. Auditing processes must be accompanied by qualification and training in order to sustainably improve social conditions.

Integration of stakeholders: Round Tables in supplier countries

The sustainable improvement of suppliers' social performance can be achieved only if the relevant stakeholders are involved. These stakeholders are predominantly governmental organizations, trade unions, business associations, non-governmental organizations (NGOs), and academic circles. Within the framework of the AVE Sector Model, Round Tables with these organizations have already been established in some important supplier countries in Asia, Eastern Europe, and Turkey. In this framework, local stakeholders discuss the results of BSCI audits, training projects, and topical issues in the field of CSR, and participate in events and workshops. Ideally, in time local organizations will chair and "own" these bodies, which are not supposed to be BSCI Round Tables controlled from faraway Brussels. In the implementation of the BSCI in the food supply chain of its member companies, Africa in particular has come more into the radius of action of the BSCI.

Besides the training projects, the Round Tables are an important element in achieving a sustainable improvement in the production sites. Establishing and guiding these bodies is not always a simple task. In some countries the open dialogue between employers, employee representatives, and the government is not an easy issue. The parties first have to develop an understanding that they are social partners approaching the topic together, discussing with each other—sometimes quite controversially—and working out pragmatic solutions. A climate of trust in the Round Tables is a solid basis for constructive discussions and successful projects. Right at the beginning, these forums in supplier countries have to be supported by European partners—and any reproach of neo-colonialism must be avoided.

On the other hand, trade unions, employers, and NGOs find themselves in a difficult situation when the government does not approach the issue of social standards in the desired manner. This is the case in Turkey, for example. Moreover, current Turkish laws make it very difficult for trade unions to take root in companies. In the textiles sector there are as many as three trade unions, which are often in competition with each other. This does not facilitate the work of a Round Table.

In countries where the government pushes the topics of CSR and social responsibility, many things are easier—but, of course, not quite everything. The Chinese government has made CSR a part of the current five-year-plan, and in 2007 it renewed the labor law. In China two issues currently present a specific challenge: first, the magnitude of the country where provincial governments and local authorities are not always committed to implementing the rules created by the central government in faraway Beijing. Second, there are so many production sites that it takes a lot of time to get a critical mass of companies actively involved.

Another obstacle is the absence of trade unions. In countries such as China or Vietnam, where there are no free trade unions, the BSCI's demand is to establish other bodies in the supplier companies which are freely elected by the employees and which have the right to negotiate with the management (so-called parallel means). Nevertheless, in China a true CSR boom can be seen. The interest in this topic is so significant that the demand for training is growing continually. Chinese producers have quickly discovered this topic for themselves—not only because of the requirements of European and American business clients. The central government has also put pressure on companies to implement legislation. Competition with India and other countries has increased the need to focus on corporate responsibility. In China, the BSCI closely cooperates with the China National Textile and Apparel Council (CNTAC), which is the former Ministry for Textiles. In May 2007, the FTA, as the legal umbrella organization of the BSCI, and CNTAC adopted a Memorandum of Understanding in order to support their respective CSR activities. In 2006, CNTAC created its own social standard for the Chinese textiles industry (CSC9000T) which, in addition to the ILO Conventions and Chinese law, refers to the BSCI as a reference. This is further proof of the growing interest in CSR among key Chinese organizations. Even if CSC9000T does not correspond to the BSCI criteria—especially with regard to freedom of association—it is still a first step in the right direction.

In India the issue of CSR is at the top of the agenda in many organizations. There are many trade unions in different regions and a large number of NGOs and consulting firms at work. In the different industrial regions of India, Round Table meetings have been held in Delhi, Kolkata, and Mumbai. A social dialogue is ongoing and companies are watching China, their largest competitor, with great interest. The improvement rate established on the basis of the BSCI re-audits has been considerably higher than in other countries. This is a positive development. However, there are some things which make the issue of social responsibility in the supply chain difficult on the Indian subcontinent. The caste system is a difficult topic, even though Indian law forbids discrimination, but the issue of child labor is the biggest challenge in India. According to recent reports, child labor is on the rise again. Often the Indian government agencies are not able to fight child labor effectively. Child labor occurs in conjunction with debt slavery. In the recent past this sad issue has featured prominently in the media. No system can guarantee that there is no child labor but efforts can be made to reduce it. It is a topic that is discussed intensely within the BSCI. An important approach to it is—as mentioned above—better transparency in the supply chain, in particular when subcontractors are involved. The cases that became known to the wider public through the media in 2007 dealt with suppliers to subcontractors of the supplier of European and U.S. companies.

This raises the question: how can greater transparency be achieved deep in the supply chain? Basic principles like "should we retain products with embroideries in our product line, if the risk of child labor in this field is high?" are being discussed. This leads to the question whether such sourcing strategies make sense at all. Should products from certain countries be boycotted? What impacts do boycotts have—do they really help? Greater transparency in the supply chain and additional training—not only for suppliers but also for buyers—are the right approaches to improve the current situation.

Yet a different situation can be observed in Bangladesh. Bangladesh is an important supplier for BSCI member companies as well as for numerous other companies. Because of the—relatively—low number of factories working for exports, more overlapping of suppliers can be seen between the importing companies than in other states. This is why supplier companies have greatly appreciated the BSCI as a joint platform of many of their business partners. In Bangladesh, the synergies tend to be higher than in other countries.

Companies importing from Bangladesh are mainly worried about accidents and fire. In 2005, the collapse of a factory, which had not been built according to building law, drew attention to the precarious nature of many factories. Due to such tragic events, many workers died or were seriously injured. Following these incidents, discussions about this were led at the stakeholder Round Table and other stakeholder forums such as the so-called Buyers Forum and the Multi Fiber Arrangement (MFA) Forum—often with the same stakeholders participating. It is a positive step that endeavors are made to push the issue of social standards as well as the issue of the unlawful building of factories. It is also worth mentioning here that these are two areas that cannot easily be combined with one another—at least not within the framework of an audit. However, it is questionable whether parallel Round Tables are very efficient. It would be desirable to align these initiatives—something that is often more difficult than it appears.

The topic of minimum wage has been under discussion for a very long time in Bangladesh. The minimum wage is considered to be too low by many stakeholders. The minimum wage was finally increased at the end of 2006. Due to this development, factory managers had to think of strategies to finance this additional expenditure. The situation was mirrored in the social audits—from the end of 2006 the performance in the field of wage compensation went down drastically. The reason was that the lawful wages paid until the end of 2006 were no longer compliant with the minimum wage after the law amendment. Here again it becomes clear that the training of management in these core issues is of major importance.

Cooperation with SAI and stakeholders in Europe

BSCI also cooperates with stakeholders at international and European levels. From the very beginning of the initiative, the BSCI has established a dialogue with NGOs, trade unions, governmental organizations, and business associations. From the start, the BSCI has fostered close dialogue and cooperation with SAI. The BSCI and SAI have signed a Memorandum of Understanding which underlines the mutual support and cooperation, particularly with regard to common training activities. In addition, the

BSCI has joined the SAI Advisory Board and the Accreditation Committee.

The dialogue with stakeholders is fruitful and constructive, and in December 2007 a circle of stakeholders joined together in order to meet regularly and to assist the BSCI openly and critically but constructively. SAI participates in this forum. The stakeholders' comments and demands help to inform the discussions and decisions within the BSCI. However, fundamental strategic decisions, such as the initiative's budget, will be reserved for BSCI members only.

Another platform of cooperation with non-BSCI companies as well as stakeholders is possible within the framework of the Supply Chain Laboratory. This laboratory is moderated jointly by the BSCI and CSR Europe, the biggest CSR business think-tank, and the Greek CSR network. Within the framework of the European Alliance for CSR, which was founded in March 2006 by the European Commission, 20 laboratories dealing with specific CSR topics have been established. With regard to the subject of supply chain, the BSCI cooperates with various companies such as Hewlett-Packard, Volkswagen, L'Oréal, and Titan, the biggest Greek producer of cement, who are the four laboratory leaders, and with other companies including BASF, Bayer, Bouygues (a French real estate company), Sony, and Toyota as well as with representatives of the Dutch government and The Copenhagen Centre as stakeholders.[2] The supply-chain laboratory works on practical instruments for suppliers and buyers which should be useful and desirable for any of these companies and beyond. The European Commission, which fosters the cooperation between companies with the participation of stakeholders, appreciates these concrete projects as well as the arising synergies.

The FTA, providing the legal framework of the BSCI, is a supporter of the UN Global Compact (UNGC) whose principles are supported and promoted by the BSCI. Like any other member of the UNGC, the BSCI has to report on its activities and projects on a yearly basis. The annual report corresponds to the GRI Guideline 3 of the Global Reporting Initiative (GRI), the recognized standard for sustainability reporting. Moreover, the BSCI is an organizational stakeholder of the GRI.

2 The webportal of the laboratory can be found at www.csr-supplychain.org.

Outlook after six years of the BSCI—a sound basis for the future

The main issues for the BSCI in the months to come are clearly defined. On the one hand, it is essential to further consolidate the system. As to system implementation, it is above all crucial to further consolidate the implementation of the BSCI module in the food supply chain of BSCI members. In this sector, the implementation follows the same approach as in the non-food sector. The management instruments have been adjusted to the specific structures and challenges in the food supply chain, which is more complex and varies more from country to country than in the textiles or hardware sectors. Moreover, with regard to primary production, there are some different legal regulations which will have to be accommodated.

Auditing will be expanded in order to see the changes in social performance after training and qualification projects. In order to allow for the important transfer of know-how, more efforts in the field of qualification are planned and necessary.

Cooperation with different stakeholders at local and European levels will be intensified further. Here, too, the issue of qualification and training will be an important element.

The BSCI will continue to forge the creation of more synergies for its members and their suppliers, increasing the circle of members and intensifying cooperation with other companies and organizations for greater harmonization.

Much has been achieved since the foundation of the BSCI in March 2003. However, it is necessary to establish and consolidate local structures in the supplier countries, so that the local companies and stakeholders can take over. The BSCI has fostered many good achievements, but there still remains a lot to be done.

8

Key performance indicators for social compliance in the supply chain

Craig Moss

Social Accountability International, United States

Integrating compliance and sourcing inside the company

The companies that take corporate social responsibility (CSR) in the supply chain seriously are those that are on the road to integrating CSR into their sourcing. The vast majority of companies send conflicting messages to their suppliers. Factory managers typically have two separate communication channels with a brand or retailer: one channel with the sourcing department, and another with the compliance department. These are examples of the contradictory messages they receive.

> "If you want the order, you've got to come down on price. No way around it."
>
> "We need to review your piece-rate calculations. It seems many workers are not making an acceptable wage."

> "I don't care how you do it, just make sure you ship on time for holiday deliveries."
>
> "I know it was peak season, but there was clearly excessive overtime again. We have to drop your social compliance rating."
>
> "Good news. The re-order quantity is 80% more than expected . . . No, I can't give you extra time."
>
> "We heard you may be using unauthorized subcontractors. We need to look at your production records. You know this is a major problem for both of us."
>
> "Hey, remember which department issues the purchase orders!"

It is one thing for a brand or retailer to have well-articulated, clearly communicated supplier codes and policies that address all of the elements of the core labor standards. It is another thing to act on them and show suppliers that they practice what they preach.

The compliance department pushes suppliers to meet social standards. They want suppliers to reduce overtime and pay a living wage. They audit to verify compliance. Then the sourcing department comes in and pushes for cheaper prices and faster delivery.

If a brand sends a mixed message, the supplier will listen to the sourcing department. Why? Because the supplier will listen to the department that is issuing the purchase order.

The only way for a brand to send a consistent message to suppliers is if there is internal agreement inside the brand on the content and tone of that message. Brands need to have complete internal agreement between the departments before they can present a unified front to suppliers. It is impossible for companies to send a consistent message to suppliers unless social compliance measurements are integrated into both the sourcing and merchandising departments' supplier evaluation system.

Supply-chain management is increasingly driven by information technology. As the supply-chain management systems become more established it will become harder and harder to integrate the compliance data in a meaningful way. CSR will be relegated to a secondary role—kept down by legacy information technology systems. It will continue for most companies as a public relations risk mitigation strategy.

Leading CSR companies are now including some type of social and environmental compliance measurement in the key performance indicators they use to measure suppliers (external) and the job performance measurement of their purchasing department (internal). The companies that make the investment now to integrate CSR into their sourcing and merchandising will gain a competitive advantage over the next decade. The effort will be worth it. This move will put a company on the path to continuous improvement in its supply chain. These are the companies that will be able to show a return on their CSR investment.

One of the challenges for senior management is to position CSR as an investment and not a cost. To accomplish this, the compliance effort must be integrated into the day-to-day operations of other departments, especially the sourcing department. Social compliance needs to be integrated into the design of the core management systems and performance measurements. This integration will help companies to build a business case for social compliance. The CSR department needs to take the lead in this effort with the clear support of top management.

Steps to integrating compliance and sourcing

For companies ready to proceed, the first step is for the CSR department to look at the information tools and measurements being used by the sourcing and merchandising departments. Examine internal performance measurements for the compliance, sourcing, and merchandising departments. Review performance measurements for suppliers.

Internally, the CSR department needs to make sure that there are no inherent conflicts in how people are expected to perform in the company. Collect the job descriptions, performance evaluations, and compensation plans from the sourcing and merchandising departments. Compare them with those of the compliance department. Look at them in light of the supplier code of conduct. Determine if there are conflicts between the departments. In many cases there are fundamental problems between the way a company operates internally and the expectations for its suppliers. If there are conflicts they need to be eliminated in order to push for change in the supply chain.

Key performance indicators (KPIs) for suppliers need to be reviewed. Typically, they measure things such as price, lead-time, on-time delivery, quality level, defect rate, and product development capabilities. Some companies are using a supplier scorecard that features a single aggregate score. Other companies are opposed to the supplier scorecard. They feel that a single numerical ranking does not capture the "soft" side of supplier performance. The supplier's flexibility, creative input, and communication responsiveness can be lost in the scorecard method. It also reduces the importance of what can be a long-standing relationship between people. Regardless of how the sourcing KPIs are measured, the purpose here is to incorporate social compliance ratings into the existing supplier KPIs. If a scorecard method is used, we recommend that the social compliance ranking account for at least 10% of the total score. Current best practice is 20% of the total score.

Now look at the social compliance performance measurements the company keeps on its suppliers. Many leading companies use a tiered rating system for measuring a supplier's social compliance performance. A tiered supplier ranking system is a pragmatic foundation and provides the best data over time for tracking performance links. Examples of tiered systems in use include:

- Three-tier (Red–Yellow–Green)
- Four-tier (Critical–Needs improvement–Good–Excellent; Excellent = SA8000-certified)
- Five-tier (1 star to 5 stars; 5 stars = SA8000-certified)

The next step is to design a matrix that intelligently overlays the social performance with the KPIs. With greater integration of information from the compliance and sourcing departments, it is possible to track supplier performance based on the level of social compliance. This tracking can be done by looking at changes in the performance of an individual supplier, or by looking at aggregated performance for all suppliers at a certain social compliance level.

Experiment with different ways of creating an integrated reporting matrix that fit the existing systems. The key is to identify and report links between business performance and social performance. Tracking the joint performance over time provides data to build the business case. Companies that started this integration two or three years ago are now starting to report a correlation between a supplier's level of social compliance and its business performance. Higher social compliance seems to mirror higher overall KPI scores.

There are so many interesting questions to track. Some examples:

1. Does on-time delivery rate improve when social compliance improves?
2. Do suppliers with a higher compliance rating have higher quality ratings?
3. Do suppliers with higher social compliance have better R&D capabilities?
4. Is there a correlation between lead-time scores and social ratings?
5. Do suppliers with higher social compliance have higher costs?

Jointly tracking business performance and compliance is a critical foundation for building the case that CSR is an investment and not a cost. More importantly, this also lays the foundation for continual improvement.

Continual improvement in the supply chain

With integrated reporting, a company can set specific targets for improvement.

In this way, integration can drive continual improvement. The CSR department needs to take the lead in working with the merchandising and sourcing departments to set annual targets to improve the aggregate performance of the supply base.

A company will need to make decisions in setting annual improvement targets and allocating resources:

1. Should it focus on reducing the number of suppliers in the lowest ranking or increasing the number of suppliers in the highest ranking?
2. Should it prioritize improving the percentage of suppliers or the percentage of purchasing volume?
3. What are aggressive, but realistic, targets for annual improvement?

Incentives form an important element of driving change. Tying the performance rating and annual bonus for the sourcing department to meeting improved social compliance by a certain percentage of suppliers and purchasing volume reinforces the unified message to suppliers. It will promote change in the company and its supply chain.

The point is to measure the aggregate performance of the supply base and to set specific, realistic targets for improvement. A company may be shocked by what it finds. It may be pleasantly surprised. Remember, this is a journey. And remember the saying: the longest journey starts with the first step. But if a company is committed to social compliance, integrating compliance and sourcing inside the company is a step that must be taken. It will benefit all of the company's stakeholders and give it an advantage in communicating its commitment to the world.

Finding the social equivalent of the carbon footprint

The CSR field has been searching for simple ways to measure the social compliance of companies and their supply chains. The environmental side of CSR has come up with the "carbon footprint." Simple. Quantifiable. Memorable. It is clear from mainstream press and word-of-mouth that there has been an increase in overall environmental awareness since the introduction of the "carbon footprint."

Social compliance in the supply chain is a highly complex issue. It is dealing with issues that are of grave importance to people's lives. It is rooted in the ongoing struggle to bring fairness and dignity to workers.

The challenge is to communicate these highly complex, emotionally charged issues to people outside the CSR field. The communication needs to be simple, quantifiable, and memorable. Plus, it needs to be credible. The challenge is to distill the measurements in a way that is credible to all parties in the multi-stakeholder community: to distill without losing the essence and to distill without forgetting the true purpose of the battle for continual improvement in the supply chain.

There are two issues at play here:

1. How does the brand or retailer manage and measure the social performance of its suppliers?

2. How do all stakeholders (non-governmental organizations, trade unions, suppliers, investors, customers, consumers, and govern-

ments) measure the social performance of the brand, retailer, or original equipment manufacturer (OEM)?

In searching for the social equivalent of the carbon footprint, I believe that the most important indicator is the degree to which a brand or retailer has truly integrated its social compliance policy into the day-to-day activities of its merchandising and sourcing departments.

The degree of integration is *the* social KPI for all stakeholders to measure a company's social compliance performance in its supply chain. It is simple, quantifiable, memorable, and credible.

The social KPI needs to measure the:

- Degree of internal integration between the compliance and sourcing departments and the related incentive system
- Consistency of communications with suppliers and the related incentive system
- Aggregated social compliance of the supply base using a tiered supplier ranking system
- Annual targets for improvement

These are the quantifiable measurements that can be distilled to create the social equivalent of the carbon footprint.

Part 2
Influence

9

MADE-BY China

A joint effort of Social Accountability International and Solidaridad in China

Janet Mensink
Solidaridad, The Netherlands

Martin Ma
Social Accountability International, China

Mark Huis in't Veld
MADE-BY

Solidaridad fashion program

Solidaridad is a Dutch development organization striving for poverty alleviation in developing countries. The organization enables sustainable production and marketing of commodities such as coffee, fruit, soy, and biomass. A pioneer in the field of fair trade, Solidaridad has been a laboratory for some of the most significant innovations in the field of fair trade including establishing Max Havelaar, the Oké Banana, and the UTZ CERTIFIED Good Inside initiative. Since 2000–01, Solidaridad has also been active in the fashion industry. Programs have been set up in Peru, India and Southeast Asia, Africa, and China.

Solidaridad

Box 9.1 Overall objective of the fashion program

The fashion program's objective is the improvement of the position of the most vulnerable links in the fashion production chain in developing countries. By building up best practices, Solidaridad aims to show that a market model based on sustainable production can be a workable model for the conventional sector and in this way promote developments in this direction.

The Solidaridad fashion program works on three intervention strategies:

1. **Direct poverty alleviation.** This includes support programs for farmers and producers (market access, technical assistance/ capacity building for sustainable production, certification, facilitating credits)
2. **Civil society building.** Developing and supporting networks of civil society organizations (CSOs) (non-governmental organizations, trade unions, etc.) to strengthen and support the development of sustainable supply chains locally
3. **Policy influencing.** This includes initiating market models (e.g., MADE-BY) or new companies (e.g., Kuyichi and Fair&Co) to set an example. Policy influencing also includes dialogue, lobbying, and advocacy with stakeholders, ranging from multinationals, brands, and standard-setting organizations to governmental organizations (North and South)

Box 9.2 Pyramid of change

Codes of conduct (whether certification, monitoring, or verification systems) form an essential part of the Solidaridad/MADE-BY program. The principle of several systems with different levels of ambition is described in the "Pyramid of Change" of Solidaridad (Roozen 2007). At the base of the pyramid, sector-wide initiatives with minimal sustainability requirements are positioned. Higher up the pyramid the growing sustainability ambition is set by individual companies and at the top by consumer labels. While the base of the pyramid reflects the mainstream approach, the top of the pyramid is for niche markets only. The three different levels of the pyramid do not compete but interact and offer different solutions to different types of stakeholder. Over time the top positively influences the base of the pyramid, creating the necessary dynamics toward higher levels of sustainability.

Within the Solidaridad Fashion program, when support on certification is given, the aim is to improve working conditions and facilitate market access to new markets requiring such certifications. Improvement of working conditions and access to sustainable markets both contribute to the overall objective of the fashion program.

MADE-BY: label for sustainable fashion

Launched at the end of 2004 by Solidaridad, MADE-BY is an umbrella label for fashion brands working on sustainability. Among the 30 brands that have joined the MADE-BY initiative are: Jackpot, Nomad, Claudia Sträter, Imps&Elfs, Kuyichi, and Edun.

MADE-BY's mission is to increase the demand for sustainably produced fashion. Supply-chain management is a key aspect of the sustainability of the brand's production chain. Supply-chain management directs, monitors, and reports on the change processes that take place behind the scenes of the brands. The method is as follows. After a brand signs the license agreement with MADE-BY, an analysis of the production chain is made. Consequently, MADE-BY works with the brand to determine improvement strategies for the future, which are set out in the action plan. MADE-BY reviews matters at the end of each calendar year to see whether the targets have been met. Results are translated into a scorecard which is published on the website and in the annual report. The action plan is adapted each year and focuses on social and environmental conditions. MADE-BY is innovative by the combination of social and environmental aspects, focusing on continual improvement by a process approach, the business-like work model, and the link with development.

Box 9.3 About MADE-BY

What do we wish to achieve?

MADE-BY is an independent consumer label for fashion companies who continually improve and are transparent about the social, economic, and ecological conditions throughout the whole supply chain of their collections.

The mission of MADE-BY is to make sustainable fashion common practice.

> "Wouldn't it be great if you could buy your favorite brand made in a sustainable manner?"

How?

- The MADE-BY label gives **consumers** the assurance that a brand produces with respect for people and planet to its best efforts
- MADE-BY offers **fashion companies** advice and support for gradually improving the social, economic, and ecological conditions throughout the whole supply chain of their collections
- MADE-BY assists **suppliers** in achieving social or environmental certification and in sourcing sustainable materials such as organic cotton by means of the MADE-BY network of farmers, spinners, and fabric suppliers

Transparency as key value: Track&Trace and scorecards

MADE-BY's Track&Trace system makes the production of an item of clothing transparent, from raw material to end-product, and in this way it can establish the origin of clothing. The underlying principle is that the production chain is made traceable as soon as improvement activities to a brand's production chain are carried out.

The system has been developed in collaboration with Historic Futures from the UK and the American organization Organic Exchange. The system is unique within the fashion world.

The MADE-BY Track&Trace consumer website is linked to this system. By using the MADE-BY Track&Trace code in or on the item of clothing, the consumer can find out, on the Internet, where and by whom the item of clothing was produced.

FIGURE 7.1 Imps&Elfs scorecard, 2007

MADE-BY

Results 2007 Imps&Elfs

Socially certified
% of total collection

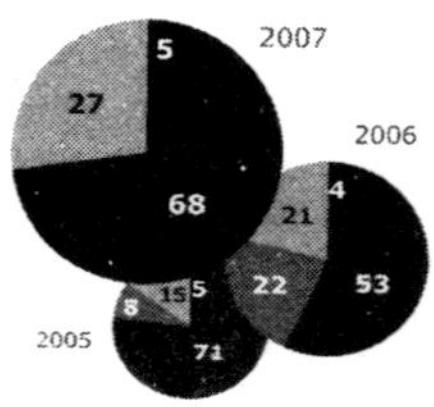

Social conditions.

Imps&Elfs has already demonstrated in the last years that it places importance on production under the appropriate working conditions. In 2007 Imps&Elfs also had a great, constant score with a slight increase in relation to last year in the two highest classifications.

Imps&Elfs also enriched its collection in 2007 with denim articles which meant working with a number of new suppliers in Turkey. These suppliers are not yet socially certified so the percentage of 'non-certified' suppliers also increased slightly.

- class A
- class B
- class C
- not certified

Organic cotton
% of total cotton collection

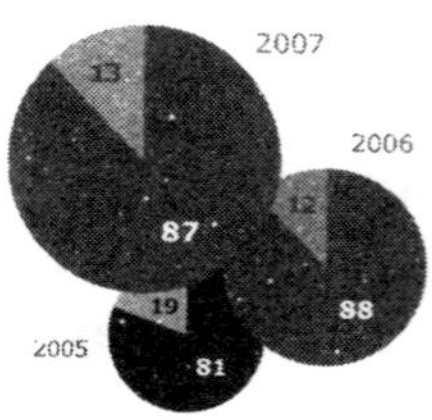

Environmental conditions.

With regard to the use of organic cotton, Imps&Elfs scored as much as 88% over the whole cotton collection this year. By concentrating on the use of organic cotton in their collection for the last three years, this environmentally-friendly solution has become standard practice in the Imps&Elfs' operation. This certainly contributed to the fact that the brand was also successful in immediately producing part of the new denim collection from organic cotton this year. Alongside working with organic cotton, Imps&Elfs is also working with their key supplier in India on a comprehensive programme to make the processing of this organic cotton as environmentally-friendly as possible by making energy and water savings and by applying for the EU Ecolabel Textiles label; the environmental standard for the production processes such as washing, dyeing and finishing.

- organic / in conversion
- conventional

Organic cotton
Kilos of cotton used

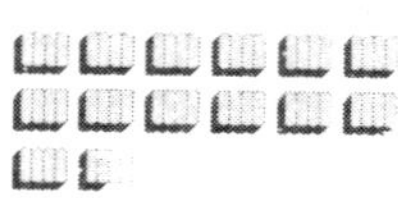

± 66.775 kilo

= 5000 kilo

Scorecards

At the end of each year, progress made by brands in the areas of environmental and social working condition are translated into two scorecards per brand (see Imps&Elfs scorecard in Fig. 7.1).

- **Social working condition.** This scorecard shows the percentage of the collection that was produced with certified suppliers. For this, a distinction is made between three classes (see the explanation of benchmark social standards below). The scorecards are accessible to all on MADE-BY's website
- **Environment.** This scorecard shows the amount of organic cotton in the previous year's collection compared to the total use of cotton in the collection. The amount of organic cotton used is also given in absolute figures (kilos of cotton used). Very soon the environmental scorecard will be extended with scores for environmentally friendly wet processing (dyeing and finishing of textile) and "green" materials, such as recycled polyester and other enviro-friendly fibers

Plans for the future

MADE-BY is working on European expansion, with offices being established in Germany and the UK in 2008 and in Scandinavia in 2009.

Solidaridad's supplier program for MADE-BY in developing countries

Solidaridad supports producers of brands joining MADE-BY in order to help them to become more sustainable by improving working conditions or by introducing environmentally friendly production techniques in their supply chains. Solidaridad also supports MADE-BY in the development of policies and tools, enabling MADE-BY to measure the sustainable achievements of its member brands. One of these tools is the MADE-BY Benchmark for Social Standards (MADE-BY 2008). In this benchmark six internationally acknowledged standards used to improve labor conditions of workers in the garment industry are rated on their system effectiveness. Their effectiveness is based on the extent to which their codes match the Joint Initiative on Corporate Accountability and Workers Rights (JO-IN)[1] code of conduct and on how they perform on other indicators including transparency, governance, and empowerment. The social benchmark is a key instrument used by MADE-BY in order to measure the extent to which a brand is producing under good social conditions. The benchmark is annually updated.

The golden rule within Solidaridad programs with suppliers (garment factories in developing countries) is that a realistic and appropriate approach will be chosen in the selection of the system used, which is tailor-made. For some suppliers a system higher in the pyramid might be relevant while for others a system lower in the pyramid will be selected. When a system with a lower level of ambition is chosen, it can serve as a stepping stone leading to the implementation of additional support programs bringing them to a higher level of social compliance over time. Note that this does not include a preference for one single system.

Most important is the fact that Solidaridad will always aim to "make a difference" with respect to the workers. We work on integral long-term improvement programs, which are never based on certification alone, but consist of additional elements such as capacity building and training, market access, improved trade conditions, and dialogue with local civil society. Solidaridad has focused on this integrated approach already and will continue to do so especially because these values-based and stakeholder-oriented approaches can contribute to higher effectiveness of the systems used. Solidaridad therefore continues with social compliance projects at the garment factory level. The program includes strengthening local CSOs on certification systems and codes of conduct and how these can be used to the benefit of these CSOs. It is our conviction that a sustainable improvement can be reached only when improvement measures in factories are set up in interaction with civil society.

1 The Joint Initiative on Corporate Accountability and Workers Rights (JO-IN) is an effort to bring together key organizations and different aspects of code implementation and/or enforcement in a program of collaborative work. Participating organizations are: Clean Clothes Campaign, Ethical Trading Initiative, Fair Labor Association, Fair Wear Foundation, Social Accountability International, and Worker Rights Consortium. Each of these organizations is involved in improving working conditions in global supply chains. The "Workplace Standards" is a joint effort to eventually converge on one code of conduct for all involved organizations.

Through its support programs Solidaridad receives practical feedback from suppliers, employees, and local civil society on the successes and failures of the different systems and codes of conduct. This includes not only good practices but also identification of limitations and cases for improvement. Solidaridad uses this input in interaction with its own stakeholders, including the standard-setting (certification/monitoring) organizations.

Joint program SAI–Solidaridad China: Treehouse case study

Since 2006, Solidaridad has had a partnership with Social Accountability International (SAI) New York for support activities in China. It started off with the objective to set up a MADE-BY flagship chain: a combination of an organic cotton project together with SA8000 certification in the field as well as with supplying factories.

Treehouse is a knitwear factory with its sales office in Hong Kong and its production facilities in Dongguan, Guangdong Province, China. The factory employs 600 workers and has an annual capacity of 800,000 pieces. With an annual turnover of €8 million ($10 million), the factory produces for leading brands in the United States and the European Union. Treehouse is a key supplier for one of the MADE-BY brands.

A team from Solidaridad and SAI began working with Treehouse at the end of 2007.

The base scan revealed the following results:

- 380 work hours per month during peak season (legal capacity 204 hours)
- One day off each month (legal four days minimum)
- Average monthly wage for core operators: €120 ($150) (legal per actual hours €200 [$251])
- Only 10% of the workforce has a labor contract (legally required)
- Only 20% of the workforce has any insurance coverage

- No worker representation
- Fines/penalties are in effect

The team did not address the social problems it found in isolation but approached and presented social compliance to the factory management as it related to the overall management of the factory. The team focused on the relationship between social compliance and human resource management.

The team conducted an analysis on the linkage between social compliance and productivity. Excessive overtime at Treehouse is partly caused by inefficient internal production systems, inadequate internal communications, and poor quality and late delivery of inputs. Overtime often leads to reduced efficiency, high accident rates, and worker dissatisfaction, and therefore high worker turnover. Improving efficiency was therefore an essential part of reducing the working hours for the workers and enhancing overall quality.

Treehouse implemented the following efficiencies:

- Investing CNY6.24 million (€624,000, $784,000) to add 47 sets of auto-knitting machines in order to replace hand-knitting machines
- Investing CNY250,000 (€25,000, $314,000) to install an enterprise resource planning (ERP) system to improve overall management, interdepartmental communication, and input planning

Although a great deal of money has been spent by management to increase the level of efficiency, this is the part of the operation that has met with the least amount of resistance. The more complex issues are those related to human resource (HR) management or the "soft skills" of the factory.

Activities in this arena involve:

1. Setting up an internal compliance/HR team to oversee the integration between compliance and business operations
2. Developing a key performance indicator (KPI) system, so that the evaluation of performance will include compliance issues, such as control of overtime, worker turnover rate, and satisfactory handling of worker complaints
3. Training of managers and workers

4. Establishing a worker committee to address workers' genuine concerns and improve worker–manager dialogue. In May 2008, 11 worker representatives were elected by peer workers, with a team from SAI/Solidaridad serving as observers. Three training sessions have been offered by Martin Ma and his team in China to the worker representatives. So far, worker representatives have been very open and willing to share their concerns. More follow-up training will be given to prepare them to engage in regular dialogue with management

While developments under items 3 and 4 are going smoothly, serious setbacks have occurred in setting up the HR team and KPI system. The HR managers hired have met with heavy resistance from the middle-management production team in the factory. Two of them have quit. A third has been fired. The implementation of the KPI system is suspended due to the turnover in the HR team.

A key brand is driving the change process. This top-down process may be at the heart of the problem of implementation. The management of the factory was extremely open and cooperative in disclosing facts and figures from the start. This helped enormously in establishing the gap between the current and desired situation and in finding ways to improve the overall situation. Changing the hard skills (machines and planning systems) was not challenging overall practices that much; changing the soft skills (setting up the HR department) is a cultural phenomenon that takes time and can meet with resistance.

Convincing management to change its management style and enable the HR team to do its work properly will take some more time. The initial target of reaching SA8000 certification in 2008 will not be met. Reaching Business Social Compliance Initiative (BSCI) compliance in 2008 will hopefully function as a stepping stone toward SA8000 certification at a later stage.

The process so far has led to the following results:

- A worker committee has been formed
- The wages have been increased to €150 ($193) per month
- Working hours are reduced to about 280 hours per month
- 100% of the workers now work under contract
- About 40% of the workers now have social insurance coverage

- No fines and penalties are levied

The Solidaridad team will continue its work within the Treehouse factory and will gradually see more results facilitated by the factory management and the brand's continuous involvement in the process.

References

MADE-BY (2008) "MADE-BY Benchmark for Social Standards," www.made-by.org/downloads/BenchmarkSocialStandards0803.pdf, accessed February 16, 2009.

Roozen, Nico (2007): "Solidaridad's Vision: A New Era," Solidaridad; www.solidaridad.nl/files/jaarverslagEN2007.pdf, accessed April 30, 2009.

10
NGO accountability
Certifying child sponsorship charities

Eileen Kohl Kaufman
Social Accountability International, United States

Social Accountability International (SAI) has been fortunate to partner with two other non-governmental organizations (NGOs) in social standards focusing on issues beyond human rights in the supply chain. SAI partnered with InterAction[1] to promote certification of NGO accountability and with Transparency International[2] on management systems for fighting bribery—the Business Principles for Countering Bribery. Like SA8000, these are also multi-stakeholder voluntary initiatives that combine management systems and norms to address social problems delivering new structures for sustaining good practices. This chapter is a report on SAI's work with InterAction to conduct a ground-breaking certification project.

1 www.interaction.org.
2 www.transparency.org.

NGO accountability

In recent years, there has been growing interest in NGO accountability and in NGOs' ability to demonstrate good governance and effective program delivery for the extremely important services provided by the voluntary sector. This reflects the increasing size, scope, and visibility of international humanitarian aid organizations and the significance and importance of their work.

Similarly, in the social standards field, SAI has worked with sister organizations in the International Social and Environmental Accreditation and Labelling (ISEAL) Alliance[3] to develop standard setting and performance guidelines. ISEAL works to define and codify best practice, at the international level, for the design and implementation of social and environmental standards systems as tools for sustainability (see Chapter 12 for more information).

Background

InterAction is the largest alliance of U.S.-based NGOs that operate in developing countries, principally in the areas of relief and development. InterAction's 160-plus members are large and small, faith-based and secular, and run the full ideological spectrum. The InterAction alliance pioneered membership standards in the early 1990s. In 1992, the members of InterAction took it upon themselves to self-monitor their activities through a set of standards—the Private Voluntary Organization (PVO) standards—out of a commitment to the highest possible performance. Since then, annual self-certification of adherence to the PVO standards has been a membership requirement. In due course, "self-certification plus" was added to the membership system, requiring members to annually not only attest but also delineate the evidence for their confidence/ assertion of compliance with the various sections of the standards.

InterAction's PVO standards strive to define good practice in the areas of international NGO governance and financial management, human resource policies, and program design and implementation, and the mem-

3 www.isealalliance.org.

bers strive to meet them and build on them. These PVO standards are not a static set of principles. Indeed, since their adoption in 1992, they have been edited, added to, and strengthened by the InterAction membership, which collectively operates in every developing country and receives billions in private contributions and government funding each year.

Child sponsorship agencies

After these PVO standards were well established, five member organizations that provide child sponsorship services undertook a pilot program for third-party certification of their compliance with the standards. SAI, and subsequently Social Accountability Accreditation Services (SAAS), partnered with these five charities and InterAction to develop criteria, protocols, training, and a certification and accreditation regime for this initiative. The five organizations—Christian Children's Fund,[4] Children International,[5] Plan,[6] Save the Children,[7] and World Vision[8]—participated in this ground-breaking project in large measure to demonstrate to their donors, their peers, their own staff, and their clients that they are walking the talk of the InterAction governance and program standards, and to identify ways to continually improve their performance and accountability. All participants realized that certification and use of standards for guiding performance are continuous processes; the documentation and measurement enable participants to see where improvements are needed and possible and to develop, document, and track improvement.

In 1999, the participants in child sponsorship certification developed additional standards for their specific work, which were ultimately adopted by InterAction's Board of Directors into the established PVO standards. In order to conduct a useful external review by a third party, it was necessary to develop consistent, measurable evaluation criteria for every section and requirement of the standards. The final product is the Child Sponsorship Certification Standards, which were used by the audit

4 www.christianchildrensfund.org.
5 www.children.org.
6 www.plan-international.org.
7 www.savethechildren.org.
8 www.worldvision.org.

teams as an objective guide to assess compliance with these standards by the child sponsorship programs of these five NGOs.

In July 2005, demonstrating a commitment to NGO accountability, the five earned certification of their compliance to these standards.

A five-year innovative project

Under the auspices of InterAction, in partnership with SAI, this group completed a five-year pilot project funded by the child sponsorship agencies and the Carnegie Corporation of New York for external third-party certification that their child sponsorship programs comply with the Child Sponsorship Certification Standards. The actual auditing process started in October 2004, after an extensive and documented self-assessment process by each NGO. Accreditation responsibilities for this program now rest with SAAS.

This is an innovative program in a number of ways:

- To date, no other charities have earned third-party accredited certification of their compliance with performance standards
- It is innovative in the structure of the auditing and certification processes: multi-stakeholder accreditation and certification panels, multi-skilled auditing teams, and a distinctive site-selection process—to make the certifications more meaningful and sound
- Importantly, it is innovative in the way the organizations worked together and learned together, sharing and seeking best practices to adapt to their individual structures and program designs

The project had several steps: document development, field testing, document revision, training for auditors and implementers, headquarters audits, field site audits, certification review, surveillance audits, guidance development, and protocol and standard revision in light of the experience during the four years. In addition, the participants periodically met to review learning and incorporate it in the program going forward. Expansion of the text of the standards included specification of the intent of each element and examples of evidence of compliance to each.

Field testing of the standards and certification methodology also served as an excellent training and learning experience for all the participants. In addition, there were formal training sessions at SAI's offices. A mock office audit at headquarters of one of the civil society organizations (CSOs) included participation by both of the certification bodies, SAI, SAAS, InterAction, and all five of the charities. Similarly, an initial field test in Honduras involved all the agencies. The process was characterized by extensive and worthwhile sharing of information and learning as the systems were tested at field sites of three of the committee organizations. After the field tests, protocols and text were adjusted to incorporate improvements identified as needed.

Next, each agency conducted a self-assessment and submitted that extensive documentation and a certification application to InterAction. InterAction assigned the auditing companies to the participants.

Audit teams

Each two-person audit team consisted of one professional social auditor and one subject-matter expert. The subject-matter experts are people with extensive experience in child sponsorship who both help the social auditor understand the work and also can put the work and issues in context. Audit reports are jointly written by the team. This is considered best practice in social auditing: combining subject matter and auditing expertise. Even though the auditors had been trained in the standards and participated in field trial audits, and even though the subject-matter experts had been trained in auditing techniques and vocabulary, neither could be as much of an expert as someone with years of experience in the topic. Similarly, in labor-standards auditing, best practice is for teams to include both systems auditors and people experienced/skilled in worker interviews, freedom of association, and other particularly thorny issues.

Auditing

This comprehensive certification process included document reviews and site visits at all five U.S. headquarters and at a sample of field offices in nine countries overall—at least three per organization. To contain costs as well as to maximize learning, the project sought to visit multiple organizations in a given country or region. Periodic surveillance audits at further field sites verified ongoing compliance during the four-year period of certification. The certification audits were conducted by teams of subject-matter experts and auditors from Cal Safety Compliance Corporation of Los Angeles (now STR) and Intertek of New Jersey. For the two audit firms, additional accreditation requirements were developed and implemented to address the specifics of this class of organization.

Sampling

The sampling methodology is innovative. It was developed to ensure that an adequate scope of sites for each applicant was seen while controlling costs. Sites were chosen from a stratified sample, to ensure that large and small, urban and remote field sites would be visited during the period of certification. For certification, at least three compliant sites needed to be reported on/visited. If one of the first three was not compliant, additional sites would be added, chosen by the auditor.

In-country visits

For certification, in addition to the five U.S. headquarters visits, field sites were audited in El Salvador, Bangladesh, Brazil, the Philippines, Kenya, Mexico, Ethiopia, Colombia, Ecuador, Guatemala, and India. Each organization has a different structure for managing and governing country programs. The subject-matter experts, among other roles, were able to bring their experience of these differing structures to the audit team enabling the teams to more readily concentrate on performance and not get held up by or caught up in background data.

The evidence reviewed and gathered was to test whether the management systems of the organization were successful in ensuring that the policies and procedures of the organization were followed at each of the numerous sites where children were served. Therefore, when the audit teams found non-conformances, the non-conformance was issued against the *headquarters*, not the local office. Confidence in service-delivery parameters at the sites not visited as well as at the sites visited—on days other than the visits—comes from confidence that the organization itself has robust systems for ensuring that field sites and partner organizations adhere to the requirements. Again, these are really important requirements—for example, each organization is required to have child protection policies tailored to its own structures and scopes.

Certification panel

This cutting-edge process is, to the best of our knowledge, the first and only such accredited certification of compliance to a set of standards by a group of international NGOs. Audit reports were submitted to and reviewed by a multi-stakeholder certification review panel which rendered the final certification decision.

The subject-matter experts involved in a given organization's audit were governed by conflict of interest rules which prevented them from auditing a firm for which they had recently worked, or for which they were planning to work in the near future. The certification panel members—a representative of a donor foundation, a subject-matter expert who had not participated in the audit, an individual who had sponsored children, and a manager of the auditing organization—had the opportunity to seek supplemental information from the audit team, from InterAction, and from SAI staff, during their deliberations on the audit report.

Every member of the panel found the process highly substantive and useful; the CSOs received thoughtful consideration and commentary on their work, far beyond a simple up/down vote. The panel had three options of findings: recommend certification, recommend certification after certain conditions are met, or note that there was not adequate information to recommend certification at this time. The panels were chaired by the certification body that would be responsible for awarding certification and conducting surveillance audits during the period of certification. This innovative, responsive group reviewed extensive documentation and audit reports, discussed the content, raised questions with the auditors who had been on site, and made binding recommendations to the certifiers.

Accreditation

The auditing organizations were already accredited to conduct social audits for SA8000; additional training and procedures were needed to qualify for certifying to InterAction's Child Sponsorship Certification Standards. Accreditation decisions were rendered by a multi-stakeholder panel, consisting of representatives of InterAction and SAI and an outside expert with decades of experience in conformity assessment issues. Since accreditation, SAAS has conducted surveillance audits of the certification bodies, by observing seven of *their* surveillance audits, in four countries.

A workshop was also convened in Washington, DC, at InterAction headquarters, for stakeholder review and comment on the standards themselves. Attendees included academics, funders, representatives of SAAS and SAI, standards experts, and others interested in NGO accountability.

Surveillance

During the course of surveillance audits after 2005, field sites in the following countries were audited: Bolivia, India, Burkina Faso, Ecuador, Nepal, Honduras, Cambodia, Philippines, Mali, Senegal, Albania, Peru, Indonesia, and Zambia. For the CSOs, depending on the size of their child sponsorship programs, program sites in between six and thirteen countries have been audited.

The surveillance audits are all at service delivery sites, in the field, and in new countries, so that a truly representative set of programs will have been reviewed during the period of certification. In this project, even more than when working with commercial organizations, there was a real imperative to economize—money going for certification cannot go for programs. On the other hand, this work is so very important that it is even more important that it be done fairly, reliably, and accountably than for the work of most organizations, be they providers of consumer or producer goods.

Comments after certification

The certified organizations attested to their feeling that the process improved their work as well as their transparency:

> The certification is further evidence that our programs are helping poor communities around the world bring lasting change to children in need.
>
> We believe the third-party review and resulting certification gives further evidence to our donors of the high quality of [our] programs.
>
> This certification means [our] child sponsorship programs meet or exceed rigorous criteria for excellence; while the process has been lengthy, the ultimate benefit to children in the developing world—now and in the future—has been well worth the wait.

> The certification provides yet another level of assurance to sponsors that their contributions are being used in the best possible ways to improve the lives of poor children.
>
> For seven years we have worked to put into place a certification process that directly addresses the public's trust in the work we do, programs that make a real difference in the lives of millions of children around the world. The end result, with its increased transparency and third-party certification of our sponsorship program, is a major achievement for our sector.

In at least two of the organizations, major aspects of the program have been adopted by the international affiliates of the U.S. agencies. This innovative program has been joined by a number of non-certification initiatives addressing NGO accountability, through research or targeted approaches to specific aspects of humanitarian organization operations. These include the One World Trust's Global Accountability Project,[9] which compares public, private, and intergovernmental multinational organizations; the Better Business Bureau; People in Aid; the Humanitarian Accountability Program; and the NGO Accountability Charter.[10]

Each of the agencies reported finding the process extremely useful, not only because of their work on documenting and implementing their own management systems, but also because of the shared learning. These organizations are truly building a community of practice in continually improving the quality of their service delivery, in serving their sponsored children and communities more successfully, more strongly, and more consciously. In 2009, when the first certification period ends, the child sponsorship organizations and InterAction will jointly determine in what ways to continue and extend the learning from the project. Additionally, the group will report back to the general membership, some of whom have expressed interest in also seeking certification of their own, non-child-sponsorship, programs.

Lessons learned

Generally applicable to other social auditing, and SA8000 in particular, are the positive results from three of these innovative techniques: support for usefulness of multi-stakeholder certification panels and for mixed audit teams. The sampling methodology seems to be a reliable and effi-

9 www.oneworldtrust.org.

10 www.ingoaccountabilitycharter.org, accessed April 20, 2009.

cient way to verify that procedures are followed in remote and numerous sites.

Going forward, at least **four interesting areas for research, documentation, and impact assessment** can be noted.

A threshold question is how to communicate the meaning of certification to stakeholders. Closely related is the question of whether there are reputation-enhancement as well as risk-reduction effects of certification.

To examine the impact of the project, field sites and national offices can be surveyed to measure how useful the process has been for the service deliverers. Also, there can be practical review of the usefulness of the root cause analysis process—exemplified in the structure of addressing corrective actions to the headquarters management system, not to the field site performance.

There is also a need to determine which aspects of this project are applicable across all the InterAction members, including those that do not operate through long-term, fixed-site offices.

And, finally, the goals of the project may expand, as during the period of certification some of the CSOs are looking for ways to incorporate evaluation of program effectiveness into the evaluation of standards compliance.

Conclusion

The child sponsorship certification audits were process and systems audits. Through our collective learning at SAI/SAAS, we now conclude that management systems are just as important for maintaining the quality and accountability of humanitarian service delivery as they are for quality and accountability of environmental or labor standards implementation or for product quality sustainability. The third-party certification process enabled all the participants to improve the quality and consistency of their oversight and provision of child sponsorship services.

References

Giunta, Kenneth (2007) "NGO Accountability in Practice," www.interaction.org/files.cgi/6095_NGO_Accountability_in_Practice.pdf, accessed February 16, 2009.

—— Interview by the author with Kenneth Giunta, InterAction consultant for the project, December 2007.

—— 'Five NGOs Set New Standard in Accountability," InterAction, August 8, 2005; www.interaction.org/library/detail.php?id=4278, accessed April 20, 2009.

Monday Developments 25.12 (December 2007; www.interaction.org/files cgi/6117_MDDec2007.pdf, accessed April 30, 2009).

Phillips, Michael M. (2005) "Big charities pursue certification to quell fears of funding abuses," *Wall Street Journal*, March 9, 2005: A1, A12.

SAI (Social Accountability International) (2007) *Ten Year Report* (New York: SAI; www.sa-intl.org/_data/n_0001/resources/live/SAI_Tenth_Anniversary_Report_HiRes2-08.pdf, accessed April 30, 2009).

11
Social Accountability International and social entrepreneurship

Morton Emanuel Winston
The College of New Jersey, United States

The twin crises of the 21st century

We live during times in which we are aware that hundreds of millions of people suffer from conditions of severe poverty, economic deprivation or exploitation, political repression, social injustice, cultural exclusion, and other kinds of human rights abuses. We are also aware that human civilization is facing an environmental crisis of historic proportions. We all know about global warming, deforestation, species extinction, depletion of natural resources, scarcity of water, toxic pollution, desertification, and a variety of other environmental threats. Many of us believe that if we do not act urgently in order to change our present unsustainable patterns of production and consumption and control the growth of the human population of the planet, our children and grandchildren who will live in the latter half of this century will be facing an environmental catastrophe of unprecedented proportions with potentially severe consequences not only for humans but also for the myriad other species with which we share the planet.

Many of us also understand that the twin social and environmental crises we are facing are linked in various ways. We know that the extreme poverty that afflicts roughly one-third of humanity is one of the causes of environmental destruction of forest lands, endangered species, and fisheries, and is a major driver of the migration of millions of poor people from rural villages to urban slums.

We also understand that the high-consumption lifestyles of people like ourselves who live in the rich world are also contributing to the global environmental crisis. We hope that the forces of globalization will promote economic development that will lift millions of people out of poverty, but we realize that it cannot follow the same pattern as was followed when our own economies developed during the last two centuries leading billions more people to emulate our Western high-consumption lifestyles, because the costs that additional burden would impose on the Earth's resources and environment would be too great to bear. So we talk about "sustainable development" and try to give this term some practical meaning. We are also aware of the fact that the rich countries can afford to do a great deal more to alleviate poverty, protect human health, promote universal education, implement human rights, preserve the natural environment, and avert a potential global environmental catastrophe than they are presently doing. There is a sense that we have reached an inflection point in history at which human civilization requires a fundamental course correction. But the political will to do it seems lacking. So, like the protagonists in a Greek tragedy, we drift toward a terrible destiny while knowing that we can avoid it, if only we could find ways to change.

If this narrative resonates at all with you, then the obvious question that presents itself is: "What am I to do?" Perhaps as individuals we accept some responsibility for addressing these twin social and environmental crises of the 21st century. Maybe we take public transport or ride our bikes to work rather than drive our cars. Maybe we decide to become vegetarians, plant gardens in our back yards, buy only locally grown organic foods, and shop for fairly traded or fairly made goods. Maybe we donate money to various charities and non-governmental organizations that work in the fields of human rights, humanitarian relief, or development, or to environmental organizations working to protect the environment, the wilderness, or endangered species.

We may do these things perhaps out of a sense of guilt (because we have so much while so many others have so little). Or perhaps out of a sense of gratitude (also because we have so much while so many others have so little). But some of us do these kinds of things because we believe that it is our *social responsibility* to do so. Those of us who think in this way choose to "take responsibility" for trying to solve some of these big problems of the world even though we do so with the knowledge that the little bit we can do in our own lives, with our own homes and families, and in the institutions and organizations in which we work, is really insignificant and will hardly make a dent on the enormous challenges human civilization is facing. Yet we do these things not because the law tells us that we must do them, but because our reason and our consciences tell us that we ought to.

Some people take this notion of social responsibility a step further by working for a non-governmental organization (NGO) or civil society organization (CSO) whose mission is specifically directed toward addressing some aspects of the twin crises. Since we understand that as individuals we cannot be very effective, we combine our talents and work in organizations that are trying to address the twin crises. In many of these organizations we often try to get governments and corporations, both of which are more powerful and better-resourced organizations than we are, to do less harm and do more good, both in the developing world and in our own societies. We fire up our computers every morning and hunt and gather information that we think might be useful in finding solutions to these problems, and put the insights we have gathered into articles, reports, and books, hoping that someone will read them who can make a difference. We fly in jet planes around the planet to meetings and conferences trading memes with other people who share our sense of social responsibility in the belief that, if we gather enough committed, like-minded people, we can create a broad-based global social movement, and through it the major institutions of society, government, and business may reach a tipping point from which real change can begin.

An even smaller number of individuals respond to their sense of social responsibility in a creative way, by envisioning and creating new social institutions designed to address one or another aspect of these twin crises. These individuals are called "social entrepreneurs," a term promoted by Bill Drayton, founder of the Ashoka Foundation, denoting "people with revolutionary ideas that could be a solution for the whole society."[1] Social entrepreneurs are what Paul Ray has called "cultural creatives":

1 See www.ashoka.org. Quoted in "The Supreme Changemaker," *Die Zeit* 46 (November 10, 2005). Translated from the German.

> Cultural Creatives tend to reject the hedonism, materialism, and cynicism generally associated with one-sided elite globalization. They are less concerned with making a lot of money, although most live comfortably. They also tend to walk their talk, three-fourths being involved in volunteer activities. On the deepest level, they are powerfully attuned to global issues and whole systems. Their icon is a photograph of the earth as a blue pearl hanging in black space. (Ray 2000)

Paul Hawken, himself a culturally creative social entrepreneur, describes a contemporary social movement of "global citizens" consisting of (roughly) 100 million people and 2 million civil society organizations, a movement with no leader, no headquarters, and no unified philosophy, that has "self-organized" itself into existence over the past decade or so, and is busily trying to jump-start the evolution of human civilization to a higher stage of integration (Hawken 2007).

Social entrepreneurs are people who have good ideas for solving some of the world's "big problems," but what really distinguishes them as a group is their social creativity: that is, their ability to organize people with complementary talents, identify and secure resources, and build organizations that allow people to work cooperatively to make change in the world.

Alice Tepper Marlin, founder and president of Social Accountability International (SAI), is clearly one of the cultural creatives. A social entrepreneur long before the term social entrepreneur was in vogue she founded the Council on Economic Priorities (CEP) in 1969 to conduct research on corporate social responsibility (CSR). In 1997 she spun off the Council on Economic Priorities Accreditation Agency (CEPAA) as a practical solution to the problem of implementing voluntary corporate codes of conduct for labor rights and human rights worldwide. Her insight was that market forces could be harnessed to drive a "race to the top" instead of a "race to the bottom" in the global workplace by "privatizing" the implementation and enforcement of global standards for labor rights and human rights developed by the International Labor Organization (ILO). The organization that she founded changed its name to Social Accountability International in 2000. Today, ten years after it was founded, SAI's SA8000 global standard is recognized as the "gold standard" in the field of workplace CSR implementation and assurance.

SA8000 and the rise of the corporate social responsibility movement

Since 1989, the year the Berlin Wall came down, and a convenient year from which to date the beginning of the current era of corporate-led economic globalization, multinational corporations (MNCs) have dramatically increased their economic power and their influence over domestic and international affairs. A convergence of technological factors including global communications networks, the rise of container shipping and air freight, computerized inventory control, and the Internet have made it economically feasible and cost-effective for MNCs to create and manage global supply chains. The globalization of production and finance has given capital a significant advantage over labor in industrial relations. More and more companies have come to see the economic advantages of sourcing production from low-wage countries with poor labor and environmental standards and enforcement, while marketing the products in more affluent societies. As a result there has emerged a "protection gap" between the observance of workers' rights in the developed and the developing countries. SAI was created in order to find a practical solution to closing this global "protection gap."

While the majority of the world's population sees globalization in a generally favorable light, many people are concerned about the power of MNCs and are worried about the harm their activities can have on society and the environment. A 2007 poll of public opinion conducted by the Chicago Council on Global Affairs found that a majority of respondents in countries representing 56% of the world's population believed that globalization is generally good for their national economies and for consumers, but they are concerned about its negative impacts on the environment and on jobs and would like to see environmental and labor standards built into trade agreements (Chicago Council 2007). Even critics of globalization will admit that increases in international trade and investment have helped to lift millions out of poverty in countries such as China and India, but many people continue to be concerned about the negative impacts of globalization on environmental quality and on labor standards, and point out that some poor countries, such as those in Sub-Saharan Africa, are being bypassed by market forces. But, where others saw globalization as a threat, Alice Tepper Marlin saw it as an opportunity to globalize labor standards.

One of the catalysts for SAI was the rise of the modern "anti-sweatshop" movement in the early 1990s, which made headlines in 1996 when Charles Kernaghan of the National Labor Committee caused TV hostess Kathie Lee Gifford to break into tears with allegations that sweatshop labor was used to make clothes for the Kathie Lee line then being sold at Wal-Mart. President Bill Clinton convened the first meetings of what was to become the Apparel Industry Partnership (later renamed the Fair Labor Association) and charged the companies he had invited to take steps to improve working conditions around the world and provide information that would enable consumers to make informed buying decisions.[2] At about this same time, Alice Tepper Marlin convened meetings of major corporations to discuss how they were combating child labor in their overseas supply chains, and these discussions in meetings held in New York and London between 1995 to 1997 led to the creation of the CEPAA whose mission was: to convene key stakeholders to develop voluntary social accountability standards based on the conventions of the International Labour Organization (ILO), to accredit qualified bodies to verify compliance with those standards, and to promote awareness and implementation of these standards globally (Leipziger 2001).

What was genuinely innovative about SAI was Alice's social creativity that enabled her to forge a consensus among a diverse group of stakeholders representing retail brand name companies, trade union representatives, auditing firms, representatives of NGOs, and academic specialists in the fields of labor rights and human rights. Individuals representing each of these groups of stakeholders formed the SAI Advisory Board, which, with the help of funds from private foundations and government grants, created the SA8000 standard in 1998. Unlike some other voluntary corporate standards for labor rights in the workplace, SA8000 is designed to be multi-sectoral, covering enterprises of all sizes and in all industrial sectors, not just apparel manufacturing. It is also designed to be a global standard that can be applied in all countries irrespective of their particular national labor laws. SA8000 does not, however, attempt to address every conceivable issue that might be placed on the CSR agenda; it focuses particularly on the observance of labor rights in the workplace and embodies auditable standards based on internationally recognized labor standards promulgated by the ILO and other UN bodies. SA8000 is

2 See Fair Labor Association History: dev.fairlabor.org/about/history, accessed February 16, 2009.

part of a system for assuring compliance with these international labor standards which also involves: training of workers and managers, training and accrediting social auditors, a management system designed to improve management practices, auditing and monitoring of particular factories and farms, complaint reporting, and the promotion of multi-stakeholder dialogue. The SA8000 certificate is awarded only to those enterprises that have credibly demonstrated to trained social auditors that their facilities are operated in compliance with the SA8000 standard. It is an achievement that testifies to the fact that a company has attained "world-class" status in its labor standards.

The brand-name retailers who join SAI's corporate involvement program commit themselves to promoting the SA8000 standard within their global supply chains and, in some cases, sharing the costs of training and auditing against the SA8000 standard. In this way, progressive, socially responsible companies can themselves "take responsibility" for doing their part to address the structural injustices that presently exist within the global system of production and, perhaps equally important, their efforts to improve labor conditions and close the global protection gap can be recognized as credible and legitimate. Suppliers benefit by enjoying better industrial relations, improved employee morale and retention, and in some cases preferential access to buyers. But the real beneficiaries are the workers in the factories and farms that have been certified against the SA8000 standard whose "human rights at work" are better protected and who are able to earn a living wage adequate to their needs.

In 1998 when SAI was founded, there were only a handful of companies that were on board with the idea of corporate social responsibility. But now there is significant uptake of the CSR agenda within the corporate sector and the idea seems to have become a standard feature of the corporate world. A recent article in the *Economist*, not the most left-leaning of business journals, published polling data showing that 59% of 1,200 business executives now think that CSR is a very high or high priority, and project that this will reach 70% by 2010, stating that, "Company after company has been shaken into adopting a CSR policy: it is almost unthinkable today for a big global corporation to be without one" (Franklin 2008). A 2006 survey conducted by McKinsey & Co. showed that more than 90% of CEOs are doing more than they did five years ago to incorporate environmental, social, and governance issues into their corporate strategies and operations, and 72% believe that CSR should be fully embedded into their operations, while only 50% think their firms are actually doing so.[3] More than half of Global 500 Companies now report on their social and environmental activities and impacts, and many have dedicated CSR officers and departments. Global corporations are now expected to have implemented management systems that allow them to comply with the relevant laws of both home and host governments as well as to internationally recognized human rights and labor rights norms, such as those embodied in SA8000. Increasingly well-managed companies engage with stakeholders as a means of learning what is expected of them and learning what works. Companies now compete with one another on CSR issues, and this "race to the top" is making change in the world by helping to close the protection gap.

SAI has played an important role in leading the CSR movement by demonstrating the truth of Mohandas Gandhi's advice to "Be the change you wish to see in the world." What SAI has been able to achieve in its ten years of existence has been remarkable. But there is still a lot more that needs to be done. Millions of workers still labor in factories and farms that have not achieved world-class status. Millions more continue to struggle in the informal economy by bartering and selling what they can to get by. Millions more barely subsist on less than $1 a day. Improving labor conditions in the global supply chain, while necessary, is only part of the solution to the problem of poverty, and poverty is only one aspect of the multiple crises that humankind needs to address and solve in the 21st century as the world becomes a global civilization. But social entrepreneurs understand that what everyone needs to do is to become "part of the solution."

There is a Chinese proverb that expresses this thought. One morning a young girl was walking along the sea shore where thousands of starfish had been washed ashore by the waves. As she walked she would bend down and pick up a starfish and throw it back into the sea. An old man saw her doing this and asked, "What does it matter if you throw a few starfish back into the sea? There are thousands of them who will still bake in the heat of the sun and perish." To which the young girl replied, "It matters to this one."

3 CSRwire, May 7, 2007.

References

Chicago Council (2007) "Poll finds international publics strongly favor labor and environmental standards in trade agreements," Chicago Council, March 22, 2007; www.thechicagocouncil.org/media_press_room_detail.php?press_release_id=59, accessed April 2, 2009.

Franklin, D. (2008) "Do It Right!" *The Economist* 386.8563 (January 19, 2008).

Hawken, P. (2007) *Blessed Unrest: How the Largest Movement in the World Came into Being and Why No One Saw It Coming* (New York: Viking).

Leipziger, D. (2001) *SA8000: The Definitive Guide to the New Social Standard* (London: Pearson Education).

Ray, P.H. (2000) *Cultural Creatives: How Fifty Million People Are Changing the World* (New York: Harmony Books).

Part 3
Impact

12

The ISEAL Alliance

Setting standards for social and environmental change

Paloma Raggo

Maxwell School of Citizenship and Public Affairs,
Syracuse University, United States

The power associated with the mainstream recognition of corporate social responsibility (CSR) as a set of productive and positive tools for social and environmental change has created both opportunities and challenges for the various stakeholders involved in setting socially responsible standards.

On the one hand, activists and non-governmental organizations (NGOs) have succeeded in creating a broader awareness of social responsibility issues. Myriad codes of conduct, standards of best practice, and accountability mechanisms are becoming increasingly recognizable and adopted by many. On the other hand, while this increased recognition has reinforced non-governmental stakeholders' presence and importance concerning issues of "good" governance, it has also heightened confusion among the general public, well-intended businesses, governments, and NGOs about which guidelines to follow and use. The International Social and Environmental Accreditation and Labelling Alliance (ISEAL Alliance) emerged as an initial response to the coordination needs expressed among labeling schemes devoted to social and environmental standards to become an international leader in setting standards for best practices.

This chapter examines the evolution of the ISEAL Alliance and the new challenges ahead. I first provide an overview of the organization's beginnings and then describe its main goals and membership.[1] I then discuss the evolution of the Alliance and foreseeable changes. Finally, I address the challenges and opportunities ahead in terms of organizational growth and governance structures.

Background

The ISEAL Alliance is an international non-profit organization which seeks to strengthen and promote the use of voluntary standards and conformity assessment as policy instruments and market mechanisms to bring about positive social and environmental change.[2] It is now recognized by various international organizations such as the European Parliament, the Food and Agriculture Organization, the United Nations Conference on Trade and Development, and WWF as the leading international organization for good and credible practices in setting social and environmental standards (ISEAL Alliance 2008). In 1999, Falls Brook Centre, a Canadian developmental NGO striving to promote sustainable forestry and farming and ecological certification,[3] brought together several independent accreditation and labeling schemes to debate the benefits of a more sustained collaboration. Leaders of these standard-setting organizations felt the need to develop a common code for standard setting, learn from the best practices of other organizations, establish which initiatives were credible against those with empty claims, and coordinate their advocacy for better practices in social and environmental standards systems. In

1 ISEAL Alliance membership has grown considerably as this chapter was written from 8 members to 16 (in January 2009). The ISEAL Alliance unveiled the public version of its new strategic plan for 2009–13 on February 10, 2009 (ISEAL 2009).

2 ISEAL, History and Mission: www.isealalliance.org/index.cfm?fuseaction=Page.viewPage&pageId=1002&parentID=490&nodeID=1, accessed February 10, 2009.

3 Falls Brook Centre, About Us: www.fallsbrookcentre.ca/about_fbc.htm, accessed February 8, 2009.

2000, during a strategic planning meeting held in New York City, participating NGOs reached a formal agreement to coordinate the advocacy activities for "socially responsible" governance practices to governmental and non-governmental audiences as well as peer-reviewed processes.[4] In 2004, ISEAL's Code of Good Practice for Setting Social and Environmental Standards was formally approved by its Board of Directors. Developing a code of best practice for standard-setting organizations was key to identifying the best procedures for achieving measurable progress toward their social and environmental objectives, while at the same time ensuring they were not creating unnecessary hurdles to international trade (ISEAL Alliance 2006: 2). By 2007, all founding members had made changes to their systems in order to comply with the ISEAL's standard-setting code. The development of a common code for best practices in setting social and environmental standards allowed members to improve their own standards by sharing and learning from each other's best practices and therefore avoiding the creation of a "lowest common denominator" standard.

The ISEAL Alliance consists of the Secretariat plus the membership. Its main goal is clearly stated: "Working together, ISEAL and its members represent a holistic movement that is changing the way the world does business."[5] ISEAL's programme of work consists of four main axes. First, it works to develop credibility tools which help distinguish and establish credible initiatives. The Code of Good Practice for Setting Social and Environmental Standards is one of its important credibility tools. The Alliance is currently developing a Code of Good Practice for Measuring the Impacts of Social and Environmental Standards, to be launched in 2010 (ISEAL Alliance 2008) and will in 2009 also begin work on a Code of Good Practice for Verification. Second, the ISEAL Alliance delivers capacity building and supports both members and emerging standards organizations subscribing to the idea that voluntary standards are an effective mechanism for achieving positive social and environmental change.[6] The Alliance seeks to build capacities and strengthen the legitimacy of its membership through technical support, research assistance, and professional development activities (ISEAL Alliance 2008a). Third, ISEAL works toward developing a framework for coordination and harmonization among its

4 ISEAL History and Mission: www.isealalliance.org/index.cfm?fuseaction=Page.viewPage&pageId=1002&parentID=490&nodeID=1, accessed February 8, 2009.

5 www.isealalliance.org/index.cfm?nodeid=1, accessed February 8, 2009.

6 ISEAL History and Mission: www.isealalliance.org/index.cfm?fuseaction=Page.viewPage&pageId=1002&parentID=490&nodeID=1, accessed February 8, 2009.

members, to ensure an accessible, comprehensive, and scalable set of tools which will be meaningful for producers, consumers, and the market alike (ISEAL Alliance 2008a). Fourth, ISEAL engages in advocacy work with various governmental and non-governmental stakeholders and participates in shaping a global movement for social and environmental standards.

A code for setting standards

The ISEAL Alliance standards build on the technical standards defined by the World Trade Organization (WTO) (Technical Barriers to Trade [TBT] Agreement, Annex 3) and the International Organization for Standardization (ISO Guide 59), further developing them to incorporate practices and requirements uniquely linked to delivering social and environmental outcomes (ISEAL Alliance 2008b). In doing so, the ISEAL Alliance aims to ensure legitimacy toward the standard-setting industry by complying with its best practices, as well as ensuring effective delivery of the social and/or environmental impacts that its members aim to achieve. The ISEAL Alliance identifies ten key elements needed for good practices in setting social and environmental standards (ISEAL Alliance 2008b). Standards must:

1. Have clear objectives
2. Be internationally defined
3. Be locally adaptable
4. Be based on law (WTO) and best practice (ISO and ISEAL)
5. Be defined clearly and consistently as well as the procedures involving them
6. Be easily accessible
7. Have a balanced stakeholder engagement
8. Have open and transparent processes
9. Be open to all interested parties, including governments
10. Be published and made freely available

Membership

ISEAL members are mainly[7] standard-setting and accreditation bodies which reflect a deep commitment to promote ecological sustainability and social justice as key business practices. As of December 2008, the ISEAL Alliance membership was composed of eight full members, nine associate members and eight affiliate members. ISEAL defines full members as "organisations that meet requirements for good practice in either their international standard-setting or international accreditation practices and that have committed to the ISEAL Alliance Code of Ethics."[8] The full members are: the Fairtrade Labelling Organization International (FLO), the Forest Stewardship Council (FSC), the International Federation of Organic Agriculture Movements (IFOAM), the Marine Aquarium Council (MAC), the Marine Stewardship Council (MSC), Rainforest Alliance, the International Organic Accreditation Service (IOAS), and Social Accountability International (SAI). Each member organization is dedicated in various ways to setting the highest standards within its field of activity. Here is a brief description of each member's main activity related to standard setting:

- "Fairtrade Labelling Organizations International (FLO) is an umbrella organization that unites 20 Labelling Initiatives in 21 countries and Producer Networks representing Fairtrade Certified Producer Organizations in Latin America, Africa and Asia. FLO is the leading standard setting and certification organization for labelled Fairtrade"[9]

- "FSC [the Forest Stewardship Council] has offices in more than 46 countries. It provides standard setting, trademark assurance and accreditation services for companies and organizations interested in responsible forestry"[10]

- The International Federation of Organic Agriculture Movements (IFOAM) is the leading standard-setting organization for organic movements worldwide. With a constituency of over 750 mem-

7 This will probably change in the future.

8 ISEAL Membership: www.isealalliance.org/index.cfm?fuseaction=Page.viewPage&pageId=486&parentID=616, accessed February 8, 2009. For a more detailed list of requirements for full and associated membership see ISEAL 2008d.

9 www.fairtrade.net/introduction.html, accessed February 8, 2009.

10 www.fsc.org/about-fsc.html, accessed February 8, 2009.

bers— from farmers' organizations to multinational certification agencies— IFOAM strives to ensure the credibility and longevity of organic agriculture as a means to ecological, economic, and social sustainability[11]

- The Marine Aquarium Council (MAC) network includes more than 2,000 aquarists, industry operators, conservationists, and researchers in more than 60 countries. The MAC is an international, not-for-profit organization that creates standards and certifications for aquarium animal collectors, exporters, importers, and retailers together with aquarium keepers, public aquariums, conservation organizations, and government agencies[12]
- Rainforest Alliance sets standards for sustainability that conserve wildlife and land, while promoting the well-being of workers and their communities. Rainforest Alliance includes over 35,000 members and supporters[13]
- The International Organic Accreditation Service (IOAS) is a not-for-profit organization established by IFOAM. The IOAS works towards conformity assessment in organic agriculture, accreditation, equivalence assessment, training, and information[14]
- Social Accountability International (SAI) promotes workers' rights primarily through the voluntary SA8000 system as discussed in this book and it is recognized as one of the most comprehensive international ethical workplace management system available to date[15]

ISEAL defines associate members as "organisations that are in the process of meeting requirements for good practice in either their international standard-setting or international accreditation practices and that have committed to the ISEAL Alliance Code of Ethics."[16] Associate members include: Accreditation Services International (ASI), the Carbon Trust, the Center for Resource Solutions (Green-e), the World Fair Trade

11 www.ifoam.org, accessed February 8, 2009.

12 www.aquariumcouncil.org, accessed February 8, 2009.

13 www.rainforest-alliance.org/about.cfm?id=mission, accessed February 8, 2009.

14 www.ioas.org/inform.htm, accessed February 8, 2009.

15 www.sa-intl.org, accessed February 8, 2009.

16 ISEAL Associate Membership: www.isealalliance.org/index.cfm?fuseaction=Page.viewPage&pageId=519&parentID=616, accessed February 8, 2009.

Organization (WFTO), until recently called the International Federation of Alternative Trade (IFAT),[17] the Roundtable on Sustainable Biofuels (RSB), RugMark International, UTZ CERTIFIED Good Inside, the Better Sugarcane Initiative, and WWF Aquaculture Dialogues. The new associate members have until 2011 to fully comply with ISEAL's Code of Good Practice for Setting Social and Environmental Standards.

Finally, ISEAL defines affiliate members as "organisations that subscribe to the ISEAL Code of Ethics and that are interested in participating in ISEAL primarily as an information sharing and awareness raising exercise."[18] These affiliate members include: Agro Eco, Chemonics International, Global Ecolabelling Network (GEN), the Institute for Agriculture and Trade Policy (IATP), the Institute for Ethical and Environmental Certification (ICEA), the International Institute for Sustainable Development (IISD), OneWorldStandards, and the Pacific Institute.

Toward new credibility tools: changes ahead[19]

After a few years of experience with the Code of Good Practice for Setting Social and Environmental Standards, it became apparent to the ISEAL Alliance that, while a code for standard-setting practices was and still is an important aspect of the legitimacy and credibility of standards system, it only represents one component of a credible system.[20] This recognition is exemplified by efforts, since 2008, to develop a Code of Good Practice for Measuring the Impacts of Social and Environmental Standards. The Impacts Code will be finalized by 2010, following which members will pool their current individual impacts monitoring efforts into a shared approach.[21] A steering committee representing various interests and stakeholders has been formed which includes representatives from NGOs, industry initiatives, research institutions, donors, and producers (ISEAL

17 The new name was adopted in October 2008: www.wfto.com, accessed February 19, 2009.

18 www.isealalliance.org/index.cfm?fuseaction=Page.viewPage&pageId=521&parentID=616, accessed February 8, 2009.

19 This section particularly benefited from a discussion with Elizabeth Guttenstein, Policy Director, ISEAL Alliance, January 19, 2009.

20 Discussion with E. Guttenstein, January 19, 2009.

21 Discussion with E. Guttenstein, January 19, 2009. See also *ISEAL Gazette* 2008: 3.

Alliance 2008c). Two main questions drive the new Impacts code: What should be measured? And how should it be measured (Rusillo 2009)? Part of the challenge is methodological. How do we collect data? What kinds of data are or can be collected if organizations operate in different fields? What key issue do we want to gather data for: poverty alleviation, capacity building, or reducing climate changes? How can we measure progress using standards setting as a tool? Finally, how do we analyze the data collected?[22] While each member of the ISEAL Alliance has gathered case studies and qualitative data on its activities and their impact on various communities, systematic and, most importantly, comparable data across field of activity and organization does not exist, yet (Rusillo 2009: 3).

Standards systems are tools to deliver social and environmental change and can be used by various stakeholders, not only by member organizations. In recent years, governments[23] and the private sector have shown an increasing interest in the use of private voluntary standards systems such as the ISEAL Alliance's standard-setting code. However, with this increased popularity comes the inevitable burden of demonstrating the impact and usage of such codes.[24] While the positive impacts are apparent and supported by qualitative data gathered by those who have worked in different fields of activity, it is challenging to translate these impacts into cross-sector, comparable, and quantitative data (Rusillo 2009). This challenges the appreciation of what role voluntary standards systems can contribute, as a whole movement, to delivering to global sustainability outcomes.

Toward new governance structures

Members of the ISEAL Alliance have recognized that their collective efforts toward developing a framework for standards systems have resulted in increasing responsibilities and accountabilities which are reaching far beyond their own organizations. The next few years will be of crucial importance for the ISEAL Alliance, as they will influence the way its credibility tools are developed, modified, and ultimately adopted.

22 Discussion with E. Guttenstein, January 19, 2009.

23 For case studies and further information see Carey and Guttenstein 2008.

24 Discussion with E. Guttenstein, January 19, 2009 .

While there has always been an open consultation process, these decisions were mainly an internal process driven by the members themselves. However, the increasing interest of various groups toward using the credibility tools developed by ISEAL has made clear that these tools impact not only member organizations but also an array of stakeholders which need to be included in decision-making processes and governance structures.[25] The ISEAL Alliance is currently developing two new structures to address these new needs. One important up-coming change in decision-making will be the establishment of a "stakeholder council." This council will be responsible for guiding the further development of codes of good practices and ultimately be in charge of adopting them, a role which was historically attributed to member organizations.[26] More broadly, the acknowledgment of multiple accountabilities requires looking into innovative governance structures for the ISEAL Alliance as a whole. As membership grows and become increasingly diverse, as does the range of those who feel they have a stake in voluntary standards systems, including government and the private sector, the next five years will prove to be crucial in thinking how to sustain in the long term such organizational growth while incorporating innovative stakeholder governance models. There are plenty of challenges ahead in designing new governance structures for a multi-stakeholder organization.[27] How should an organization with core founding members integrate a new and diverse membership? How should the board be structured to be representative of the membership but loyal to the core mission of promoting social and environmental change? Are all accountabilities to various stakeholders equal? Finally, as a movement composed of organizations that stepped in where governments would not intervene, how can ISEAL balance its involvement with governments while preserving flexibility and autonomy from cumbersome bureaucratic institutionalization of its credibility tools?

Critics could argue that the ISEAL Alliance is just another "club" of organizations, in this case mostly labeling organizations, whose main goal is promoting the self-interest of its members. The willingness of member organizations to change and improve their standards practices through communities of practice and learning challenges the idea that the ISEAL

25 Discussion with E. Guttenstein, January 19, 2009.

26 Discussion with E. Guttenstein, January 19, 2009. For up-to-date details on the new governance structures, please refer to ISEAL Alliance Strategic Plan 2009–2013, to be published in 2009.

27 Discussion with E. Guttenstein, January 19, 2009 .

Alliance operates out of self-interest. The standards being developed are considered as a form of public goods and are available to the general public. Furthermore, ISEAL's willingness to acknowledge that its stakeholders are not limited to its membership but also include those affected by the standards is at odds with standard-setting organizations such as the ISO. For ISEAL establishing standards is not a business in itself and profit is not a driver; instead the ultimate goal is social and environmental progress. The ISEAL Alliance's multi-stakeholder approach in engaging with organizations already involved in a sector of activity and stakeholders affected by the standards distinguishes it from organizations such as the ISO. Over the past few years, the ISO has made efforts in the field of social responsibility and has engaged with communities of practice in developing the ISO 26000 guide to be launched in 2010 (see Chapter 14). The document's purpose, however, is not to offer a new certification but to propose voluntary guidelines without including any requirements for verification and certification.[28] With this initiative, the ISO, while striving for better social responsibility, is adding yet another guide on what practices should look like without furthering the development of impact assessment and credibility tools. The ISEAL Alliance's contribution to good practices in standard setting is undeniable but ISEAL's future contributions on new ways to think about assessing impacts, involving and identifying stakeholders, designing governance structures, and expanding accountability mechanisms will undoubtedly be even more fascinating

References

Carey, Christine, and Elizabeth Guttenstein (2008) *GUVS—Governmental Use of Voluntary Standards: Innovation in Sustainability Governance* (R079 October 16, 2008; London: ISEAL Alliance; www.isealalliance.org/document/docWindow.cfm?fuseaction=document.viewDocument&documentid=745&documentFormatId=1560, accessed April 30, 2009).

ISEAL Alliance (2006) *ISEAL Code of Good Practice for Setting Social and Environmental Standards* (P005-Public draft version 4; Oxford, UK: ISEAL Alliance; www.fairtrade.net/fileadmin/user_upload/content/P005_ISEAL_Code_PD4_Jan_06.pdf, accessed February 8, 2009).

28 ISO Social Responsibility: isotc.iso.org/livelink/livelink/fetch/2000/2122/830949/3934883/3935096/home.html?nodeid=4451259&vernum=0, accessed February 19, 2009.

—— (2008a) *Introducing ISEAL Factsheet* (Factsheet E035 October 10, 2008; London: ISEAL Alliance; www.isealalliance.org/document/docWindow.cfm?fuseaction=document.viewDocument&documentid=733&documentFormatId=150).

—— (2008b) *Standard-Setting Code Factsheet* (Factsheet E037 November 28, 2008; London: ISEAL Alliance; www.isealalliance.org/document/docWindow.cfm?fuseaction=document.viewDocument&documentid=751&documentFormatId=1505).

—— (2008c) *Impacts Steering Committee Terms of Reference* (A093 September 29, 2008; London: ISEAL Alliance; www.isealalliance.org/document/docWindow.cfm?fuseaction=document.viewDocument&documentid=728&documentFormatId=1392).

—— (2008d) *P006 Membership Application Procedures: Public Draft 15—June, 2008* (London: ISEAL Alliance; www.isealalliance.org/document/docWindow.cfm?fuseaction=document.viewDocument&documentid=211&documentFormatId=1380).

—— (2009) *ISEAL Alliance Strategic Plan 2009–2013* (E058 February 18, 2009; London: ISEAL Alliance; www.isealalliance.org/document/docWindow.cfm?fuseaction=document.viewDocument&documentid=778&documentFormatId=1627).

ISEAL Gazette (2008) *ISEAL Gazette* 6.1, November 2008; www.isealalliance.org/document/docWindow.cfm?fuseaction=document.viewDocument&documentid=750&documentFormatId=1532.

Rusillo, Aimee (2009) *Public Summary: State of the Art in Measuring the Impacts of Social and Environmental Standard Systems* (R081 January 14, 2009; paper prepared for ISEAL; London: ISEAL Alliance; www.isealalliance.org/document/docWindow.cfm?fuseaction=document.viewDocument&documentid=774&documentFormatId=1616).

13

Evaluating the impact of SA8000 certification

Michael J. Hiscox and Claire Schwartz
Department of Government, Harvard University, United States

Michael W. Toffel
Harvard Business School, United States

The need for evaluation

The Social Accountability 8000 Standard (SA8000), along with other types of certification standards and corporate codes of conduct, represents a new form of voluntary "self-governance" of working conditions in the private sector, initiated and implemented by companies, labor unions, and non-governmental activist groups cooperating together. There is an ongoing debate about whether this type of governance represents real and substantial progress or mere symbolism. Advocates promote SA8000 and similar codes as a necessary tool to improve workplace conditions, especially in nations that lack robust enforcement of regulatory standards.

Many detractors worry that codes place too much emphasis on process rather than performance, and note that to be effective such codes require scrupulous monitoring by reliable and credible third-party organizations. While SA8000 has more stringent and specific requirements than many alternative codes, critics have questioned the qualifications and training of the auditors Social Accountability International (SAI) authorizes to monitor compliance with the code (Labour Rights in China 1999). Similar concerns have been voiced about auditors monitoring compliance with alternative codes, including those administered by the Fair Labor Association (FLA) and the Worldwide Responsible Apparel Production (WRAP) (see, for example, O'Rourke 2000). The manager of one auditing organization authorized to certify factories to SA8000 in China stated in 2000 that "Right now, in labour-intensive industries in southern China, the SA8000 standard cannot be enforced effectively. . . . The factories always find a way around the auditors" (Ehrlich 2000). Some critics worry that effective monitoring is not possible using commercial (for-profit) auditors like the ones authorized to audit SA8000 thus far (Maquila Solidarity Network 2001). Although many of these were raised in the years immediately after SA8000 was first published in 1997, concerns about the integrity of the monitoring process persist (Applebaum 2005). More recently, critics have questioned the potential effectiveness of SA8000 given the lack of guidance available to implement key requirements such as stakeholder engagement (Gilbert and Rasche 2008). There are real concerns that SA8000 and other types of codes might be adding to the costs of doing business without fundamentally improving social or environmental outcomes.

To date, the debates about the impact of private governance of working conditions have been dominated by philosophical and political discourse because the SA8000 and similar codes have yet to be subjected to systematic evaluation (see O'Rourke 2003; Esbenshade 2004; Vogel 2005). Very little empirical evidence is available to indicate whether those companies that have adopted such codes offer significantly better working environments in terms of safety, health, freedom of association, and fair pay practices. Almost no systematic evidence exists to indicate whether independent organizations such as SAI have been able to establish effective monitoring programs that ensure compliance with their codes, or whether they are simply being used as political cover for businesses hoping to avoid further scrutiny from activists and negative publicity. In addition, we have no rigorous evidence on whether adopting SA8000 or similar codes has any positive or negative impacts on staff turnover and absenteeism, product defect rates, sales growth, order size, and other measures of business performance.

We are aware of no evaluations, before this edited volume, that have sought to examine whether and how adopting SA8000 affects workplace practices or business outcomes. Until the results of rigorous evaluations of SA8000 are published by independent researchers, preferably in peer-reviewed academic journals, the debates about the effectiveness of the code will continue. New research that meets the highest methodological standards is critical for resolving these debates. In addition, rigorous evaluation studies can highlight areas on which to focus efforts to improve existing standards and procedures, perhaps revealing that SA8000 certification has been more effective in dealing with some types of issue than others, for example, or that it has been more effective in some industries or countries than in others.

In this chapter, we review prior evaluations of other private codes governing workplace conditions including Ethical Trading Initiative (ETI)'s Base Code, Nike's Code of Conduct, and Fair Trade. These have taken the form of focused studies examining only producers that have adopted a specific code, and comparative studies that compare code adopters to non-adopters. We then discuss several principles and techniques well known as best practices for evaluation studies in other domains. We believe there is a critical need to incorporate these principles and techniques in future evaluations of codes such as SA8000 to bolster their robustness and enable researchers to make clear causal inferences, distinguishing the performance differences between code adopters and non-adopters before adoption ("selection effects") and the performance differences that emerge after adoption ("treatment effects").

Evaluation studies: a review of existing research[1]

Have other voluntary private codes governing workplace conditions like SA8000 really improved labor standards in the places in which they have been adopted? What impact do these codes have on business performance? To date, the research aimed at answering these questions has assumed two forms. First, various **focused studies** have examined evidence from a set of producers (companies, factories, and farms) that have adopted a particular voluntary code or standard, aiming to evaluate

1 Although outside the scope of this chapter, for reviews of studies evaluating codes, standards, and government voluntary programs regarding environmental issues, see Bennear and Coglianese 2005; Coglianese, Nash, and Borck 2008; Darnall and Sides 2008; King and Toffel 2009.

compliance with that code and to describe the processes through which the adoption of the code might have affected practices and outcomes. Some of these studies examine quantitative data on a large number of code-adopting producers, while others provide more finely detailed, qualitative descriptions of the ways in which a code can affect producers. Second, somewhat fewer **comparison studies** have attempted to measure the impact of a particular code or standard by examining differences in statistical measures of standards and outcomes gathered from producers that have adopted the code and from producers that have not adopted the code. Both of these methods involve non-experimental research designs that place serious limits on the degree to which they can be used to make causal inferences about the impact of private governance.

Focused studies: producers that have adopted a particular code

Barrientos and Smith (2006) provide one of the most extensive studies of producers that have adopted a voluntary code, examining British companies participating in the Ethical Trading Initiative (ETI). The study aims to evaluate the impact of the ETI's Base Code on labor standards (e.g., health and safety standards and compliance with minimum wage laws) and rights of workers to organize and bargain collectively with employers. The ETI Base Code formally prohibits forced labor, child labor, discrimination, harsh or inhuman treatment, and excessive hours of work, and guarantees safe and hygienic conditions, regular employment, a living wage, and freedom of association and the right to collective bargaining.

The Barrientos and Smith study combines a survey of 29 ETI member companies with more detailed case studies of 23 supplier facilities located in Britain, South Africa, India, Vietnam, and Costa Rica. The researchers interviewed managers at the 29 member companies, reviewed annual reports, and asked each company to complete a survey by email. In each supplier case study, researchers conducted interviews with workers, managers, trade union officials, and representatives of other non-governmental groups and government agencies and asked each group about the impact of the ETI code. The authors report that greater compliance with the ETI code among suppliers is associated with more proactive management approaches to code implementation among buyers and the leverage held by such buyers (in terms of the percentage of supplier output they account for and the duration of the supply relationship). The interviews with workers indicated that, in general, the ETI code had led to some improvements in health and safety standards, minimum wage compliance, benefits, and working hours, but little or no improvement in terms of freedom of association and rights to collective bargaining and protection against various types of discrimination. The authors note that the mechanisms for monitoring compliance with the code often rely on firms that specialize in technical or financial audits and are better suited to identifying the visible aspects of code compliance, such as health and safety measures, than less visible aspects related to workers' rights and discrimination. Barrientos and Smith argue that this weakness is compounded by the fact that auditors often collect information primarily from management, without significantly engaging workers.

Locke, Qin, and Brause (2007) examine the workplace conditions of Nike's suppliers, all of which have agreed to comply with Nike's Code of Conduct, which "directs them to respect the rights of their employees, and to provide them with a safe and healthy work environment."[2] The authors analyze quantitative data on the working conditions among some 800 suppliers in 51 countries, gathered by Nike's own internal auditing system. The data reveal higher audit scores at suppliers that were visited more frequently by Nike production specialists and that were located in countries with stronger regulations and legal institutions. Better working conditions were also associated with smaller plant size and with more formal partnership ties with Nike. Working conditions were generally worse in facilities in Asia compared with those located elsewhere. The audit data suggest that, in general, working conditions among all Nike suppliers have improved only slightly over time. The authors also note that data from Nike's separate "compliance rating program" (which assigns simple letter grades to suppliers based on their overall compliance with health, safety, labor, and environmental standards) indicate that working conditions at more than 80% of the firm's suppliers have either remained the same or fallen over time.

A follow-up study by Locke and Romis (2007) examined evidence from detailed case studies of two of Nike's supplier facilities in Mexico (see also Locke, Kochan, Romis, and Qin 2007). The authors chose two facilities that were very similar in terms of their size, location, product line, and place in Nike's supply chain, but were noticeably different in terms of

2 Nike Responsibility Governance, www.nikebiz.com/responsibility/cr_governance.html (accessed February 16, 2009).

working conditions (wage levels, work hours, and employee satisfaction). After visiting the facilities and conducting numerous interviews with managers, workers, and representatives of non-governmental groups, the authors attribute this divergence in work conditions to differences in work organization and human resource management. Specifically, they argue that the introduction of lean manufacturing techniques in one factory had led to larger investments in worker training and greater work autonomy, raising productivity and improving working conditions at the same time.

In addition to these studies of corporate codes of conduct in the manufacturing sector, several scholars have examined evidence on the impact of Fair Trade certification among selected sets of agricultural producers. One prominent example is the study of nine Fair Trade-certified coffee cooperatives in Costa Rica conducted by Ronchi (2002), based on interviews with managers and farmers in each of the cooperatives and evidence from documents (e.g., accounting reports) generated by the cooperatives and the national Costa Rican coffee growers' consortium, Coocafé. The study reported that these cooperatives had benefited from participation in the Fair Trade system in financial terms, receiving a higher and more stable price for their coffee, and also in non-financial ways, enjoying more support for building organizational capacities. Similar conclusions were reported by researchers who interviewed farmers in seven Fair Trade-certified coffee-grower cooperatives in Mexico, Guatemala, and El Salvador (Murray, Raynolds, and Taylor 2003, 2006; Raynolds, Murray, and Taylor 2004). The study suggested that, among the non-financial benefits of participation in the Fair Trade system, increased social stability and greater access to technical training and education were particularly important for these coffee farmers.

All these studies are similar in that they focus on one set of producers (factories or farms) that has adopted a particular voluntary code or standard. They provide richly detailed descriptions of the methods by which specific codes have been implemented and the mechanisms by which codes can succeed or fail in improving working and living conditions. However, these studies are extremely limited in their ability to measure the impact of a particular code on outcomes because they lack control or comparison groups—producers that have *not* adopted the code in question, but are otherwise virtually identical to the producers that have adopted the code—the experience of which can be compared with that of the code adopters.

Comparison studies: producers that have adopted a code vs. others that have not

Weil and Mallo (2007) examine the impact of private monitoring of labor standards by manufacturers in the American garment industry. It is not a study of the impact of a voluntary code or standard, but it does assess one aspect of private governance in the form of private monitoring. The program examined in the study is a novel combination of a government regulation (and enforcement power) and private monitoring. The Wage and Hour Division at the U.S. Department of Labor is the government agency in charge of enforcing workplace standards regulations, as enacted in the Fair Labor Standards Act (FLSA). When the division discovers a violation of the FLSA at a contractor doing assembly work for an apparel manufacturer, it has the power to embargo sales of goods from that contractor. Faced with such an embargo, manufacturers enter into agreements with the division to monitor their contractors, remediate violations, and notify the division of non-compliance. Weil and Mallo study the effect of these monitoring agreements on compliance with minimum-wage laws based on data from four division surveys of around 70 apparel contractors (randomly selected from all manufacturing and contractor firms appearing on the California and New York registration lists between 1998 and 2001). Except among the New York contractors surveyed in 2001, the results indicate that contractors subject to monitoring by manufacturers had substantially higher compliance with minimum-wage laws when compared with contractors not subject to such monitoring.

Nelson, Martin, and Ewert (2007) have examined the impact of several different codes of conduct in the South African wine and Kenyan cut flower industries. In South Africa, the authors compared five wine companies that had adopted the code of practice of the Wine and Agricultural Ethical Trade Association (which is broadly similar to the ETI code) with 15 companies that had not adopted the code. In Kenya, they compared six farms that had adopted any of a variety of codes that address labor practices and environmental standards (including those of the Kenya Flower Council, the Flower Label Program, and Fair Trade) with six farms that had not adopted any such code. The study finds that, compared to workers in the non-adopting enterprises, workers in code-adopting companies and farms experienced better material conditions (e.g., wages, working hours, and housing quality) and better social conditions (e.g., daycare facilities, access to HIV/AIDS education, and medical care). Overall, the study reports that the adoption of codes of conduct is associated with better working conditions in both industries, although the effects are not always large and are less pronounced for casual workers.

Perhaps the most ambitious comparison study aimed at measuring the impact of Fair Trade certification has been provided by Arnould, Plastina, and Ball (2007). The study was based on a survey of more than 1,200 certified and non-certified coffee farmers in Peru, Nicaragua, and Guatemala (see also Plastina and Arnould 2007). In each of the three countries, the researchers surveyed a random sample of farmers from within a sample of certified coffee-growing cooperatives, and then surveyed a random sample of non-certified coffee farmers in areas adjacent to those cooperatives. The certified and non-certified groups were then compared. The study reports that the Fair Trade-certified farmers generally received higher prices and sold larger quantities of coffee than non-certified farmers, and also appeared to enjoy a slightly higher material quality of life (in terms of access to water, medical care, cement floors, etc.) and higher levels of self-reported well-being. Certified farmers also appeared somewhat better off than their counterparts in terms of education and health levels within their families. Becchetti and Constantino (2006) used a similar comparison approach in a smaller study involving a survey of 120 Fair Trade certified and non-certified fruit farmers in Kenya. They report that certified farmers appear to have greater satisfaction with prices and incomes, greater crop diversification, and higher food consumption and dietary quality than non-certified farmers.

These types of comparison study provide a first step toward assessing the impact of particular voluntary codes (and private monitoring programs). However, as discussed further below, they, too, suffer from severe methodological limitations, the most important of which is **selection bias**. To make causal inferences, it is not sufficient to simply compare working conditions and outcomes between existing producers already participating in the code in question and producers not participating in the code. Because one group is participating in the code and one group is not, these two groups are likely to differ in many observed and unobserved ways that could explain any difference in outcomes between them.

Evaluation design: general principals for impact studies

The remedy for the methodological problems encountered in standard-focused and comparison studies of voluntary codes lies in better research design. Robust evaluations should incorporate three fundamental research design principles: (1) examine performance over time; (2) compare the performance of participants to that of a very similar set of non-participants; and (3) address selection bias using randomized trials wherever possible. We describe general guidelines for designing impact studies below.

Examine performance over time

Studies that simply compare the performance of producers that have adopted a particular code to that of non-adopters at a particular moment in time may well find significant differences between the groups in terms of performance. Such cross-sectional studies have several attractive features including the ability to survey or interview managers and staff at these companies in a compressed time-frame. However, these types of studies have a fundamental design weakness when it comes to evaluation: one cannot learn whether performance differences between adopters and non-adopters actually arose due to the adoption of the code, or whether the differences observed were already evident even before the producers decided whether or not to adopt the code. For example, some producers that adopt SA8000 might do so because they already have implemented strong work conditions, find it relatively easy to conform to the standards requirements, and thus need to make few subsequent changes to their operations. On the other hand, some producers adopting SA8000 might do so to drive improvements in their operations using the standards as benchmarks to be achieved. It is possible that, in both of these cases, a year after adoption, adopters might outperform non-adopters. However, research designs that involve comparing the performance of adopters to non-adopters only in the post-adoption time-frame are unable to distinguish between these two very different scenarios (referred to as "selection effects" and "treatment effects," respectively).

Ideally, evaluations should gather data from all organizations in the sample before a substantial number of them adopt the code, and again afterwards. Data should also be gathered from non-adopters at the same times (the importance of including non-adopters in any evaluation study is described in the next section).

Pre-implementation data

Gathering baseline data is an essential part of evaluation. Researchers should collect data on as many important producer characteristics as possible, and on all of the outcome or performance indicators that will be used in the evaluation. The important issue here is that these data are collected *before* the code is adopted by a substantial number of the producers in the sample, making it possible to distinguish between selection and treatment effects in the analysis.

Post-implementation data

The follow-up survey should be conducted well after the period during which producers adopt the code, and should measure all the same producer characteristics and outcomes measured in the baseline survey. By gathering the same types of data in the baseline and follow-up surveys, both across- and within-group differences can be examined, making the causal inferences more robust.

The importance of examining non-adopters

Examining only the performance of participants in a code seldom produces convincing evidence of the impact of adopting the code. If one examines only companies and suppliers subject to the ETI Base Code, for example, without considering how these firms compare with counterparts that have *not* adopted the code, it is impossible to make any valid causal inferences about the impact of the code. How do we know what would have happened among the ETI companies and firms if they had not been part of the ETI system? Even if one can show that there has been very little improvement over time in workplace standards among suppliers subject to Nike's Code of Conduct, to switch to another example, if we do not know what occurred among similar suppliers that were *not* subject to the Nike code, it is extremely difficult to say anything about the impact of the code.

Imagine a study that tracked the performance of organizations that adopted SA8000 in 2003 and found that their performance was steady from 2001 to 2003, and then improved dramatically from 2003 to 2005. Although it would be tempting to conclude that SA8000 adoption was responsible for this improvement, such a conclusion would be unwarranted. After all, non-participants might also have experienced improvements since 2003 due to factors having nothing to do with SA8000 adoption, such as economic cycles and inflation, changes in the labor market, new regulations, changes in regulatory enforcement, or the availability of new technologies.

To be much more confident that performance changes are associated with the code being studied, researchers need to compare the performance of code adopters to that of non-adopters over time. That said, the inclusion of non-adopters and temporal data in an evaluation provides necessary—but not sufficient—conditions for generating convincing causal inferences, as explained in the next section.

Note that our focus has been on the problem of selection bias when comparing outcomes between code adopters and non-adopters as the first-order research design issue. A separate methodological issue is the possibility of "contamination bias" if treatment effects among code adopters actually spread or spill over to influence outcomes among non-adopters. It is possible, for instance, that improvements in business outcomes among code adopters might lead nearby non-adopters to alter their own practices and improve their performance, emulating the behavior of adopters without actually signing on to the code. In this scenario, a comparison between code adopters and non-adopters would actually underestimate the impact of the code. Spillover effects might also work in the opposite direction. If code adopters lay off underage workers, for instance, reducing demand for these workers in the local labor market, local non-adopters might adjust by relying more on these underage workers or by providing their workers with lower wages and worse conditions. In this case, a comparison between adopters and non-adopters would overstate the impact of the code on labor standards. Methodological strategies for addressing contamination bias include the careful selection of control groups to minimize the chances of spillover effects, and direct measurement of adaptive forms of behavior among the units being studied.[3]

3 A detailed review of methods to avoid or accommodate contamination bias is beyond the scope of this chapter.

Overcoming selection bias

To make causal inferences, as noted above, it is not sufficient to simply compare the performance of adopters to the performance of an arbitrary group of non-adopters, as these two groups are likely to differ in many ways that could explain any difference in outcomes between them. To examine the causal effect of Fair Trade certification on farmer income, for example, it is not sufficient to simply compare the incomes of certified and non-certified farmers because the two groups are likely to differ in terms of many other characteristics—such as farming skills, innovativeness, ambition, risk acceptance, etc.—that could help explain why they have decided to join the Fair Trade program or not, and could also independently explain any difference in incomes between them.

This point can be illustrated with a simple example. Assume coffee farmers are of two types: low skill and high skill. Assume that the high-skilled farmers achieve higher incomes. If the high-skilled farmers tend to select into Fair Trade certification, then a simple comparison would find that certified farmers are better off than non-certified farmers, even if certification itself had zero impact on incomes. The difference in incomes could be entirely driven by the difference in skills between the two groups of farmers. Here, the selection bias can lead to a very wrong inference, with all the difference in income falsely attributed to the Fair Trade program and not to the true cause (farming skills). It need not be skill differences, of course, but any of a large set of characteristics, many of them extremely difficult to observe and measure.

It is worth noting that selection bias can undermine attempts to measure the impact of a program even if participation in the program is not voluntary. In the case of the private monitoring program in the U.S. apparel industry, for instance, manufacturers and contractors did not voluntarily select themselves into the program: entering into a monitoring agreement (covering all its contractors) was mandatory for a manufacturer sourcing from a contractor found to be in violation of existing labor laws by the Department of Labor. Selection bias still makes any evaluation of the impact of the program very difficult. The manufacturers that had been caught sourcing from a contractor that violates labor laws and compelled to sign a monitoring agreement are actually likely to differ in many ways from counterparts that have not been in this position. Some of these differences might reflect managers' attitudes about the importance of labor standards, or expectations that the firm will be targeted for government inspections in the future. These kinds of difference between the two groups might have large effects on compliance with labor standards, and it is very difficult to account for all such differences.

Below, we describe three alternative research design approaches that can provide ways to overcome selection bias in evaluations of codes such as SA8000: (1) randomization; (2) matching to establish quasi-control groups; and (3) using instrumental variables. The first two approaches provide alternative methods that attempt to compare code adopters to non-adopters that are as similar as possible in every way except for the fact that they did not adopt the code. The third approach, most commonly used in economics, involves identifying a measure that meets a unique set of criteria for eliminating selection bias effects in statistical analysis when randomization and matching designs are impossible.

Randomization

The ideal research design for evaluations would incorporate the use of randomized trials to create "treatment" and "control" groups. This is the critical methodological principle guiding the best new research evaluating policy programs and interventions associated with development and poverty alleviation.[4] Why is randomizing so helpful? Random assignments of individuals or organizations to the intervention, such as randomly assigning producers to adopt a code of conduct, will create groups that are essentially identical on all observed and unobserved characteristics. This approach completely overcomes concerns that organizations that voluntarily sought the intervention (e.g., adopted the code) differ in important ways from those that did not. With random assignment, any difference in outcomes can be directly attributed to the intervention of interest.

There are creative ways to apply randomization even in situations in which it might seem impractical. In particular, if the actual treatment cannot be randomized, randomized encouragements to get treated can often be used. For research on the adoption of a specific voluntary code, it might be impossible to randomly assign code adoption to producers, but it might be possible to randomize some form of encouragement to adopt a code such as SA8000 (e.g., training seminars, consultations, etc.).

There are also ways to apply randomization in cases in which it might

4 For example, all research sponsored by the Massachusetts Institute of Technology (MIT) Poverty Action Lab incorporates randomized trials (see www.povertyactionlab.com).

not seem fair or ethical to randomly assign potentially beneficial treatments among needy subjects. This might be an issue when designing a study with encouragements to assist small farmers or firms to adopt a code or standard (e.g., Fair Trade). One simple approach in these types of cases involves randomization in the *order* in which the encouragements are administered among farmers (i.e., creating early and late treatment program groups), with all receiving the same assistance over time.

Although experiments with random assignment represent the "gold standard" of evaluation design, they are not feasible when seeking to evaluate the impact of codes on organizations that have already voluntarily adopted them. Furthermore, random assignment is often only implemented after the program administrator is convinced of its merits by a researcher, which is not always possible due to a conflict of interest that sometimes arises. Whereas program evaluators are interested in understanding the conditions under which the program is effective, program administrators are often most interested in deploying the code as rapidly and broadly as possible. Depriving some potential adopters of adopting, or even intentionally delaying some applicants, in order to randomly assign them to a control group might sometimes be at odds with the goal of rapid diffusion.

Beyond questions of feasibility, experiments sometimes require substantial patience. Even in cases in which researchers successfully convince program administrators to engage in random assignment, researchers might need to wait months or years before post-assignment performance data become available. Indeed, the World Bank notes that:

> Randomized evaluation designs, involving the collection of information on project and control groups at two or more points in time, provide the most rigorous statistical analysis of project impacts and the contribution of other factors. But in practice it is rarely possible to use these designs for reasons of cost, time, methodological or ethical constraints. (World Bank 2004)

Fortunately, two other approaches can yield robust evaluations, although each one requires important assumptions and has its own limitations. We turn to those now.

Matched control groups

Recall that the purpose of randomization is to create a group of organizations that adopted a particular code that possesses the same characteristics as a group of organizations that did not adopt the code so that the performance of both of these groups can be tracked over time, ideally before and after the former group actually adopts the code. As already alluded to, the challenges to implementing randomization are often large, and sometimes insurmountable. Fortunately, researchers can alternatively identify a "matched" group of non-adopters with characteristics very similar to those of the adopters. This technique requires two things of the researcher: (1) to have a thorough understanding of the factors that lead organizations to voluntarily adopt the code; and (2) to have access to data on many—ideally all—of these factors. Matching is a widely used approach in evaluations conducted by academics. Researchers can sometimes identify one or more non-adopters with characteristics that are virtually identical to each adopter ("exact matching"). Even when exact matches are not available, researchers can apply statistical techniques (e.g., "propensity score matching") to create groups of participants and non-participants that, as a whole, are very similar.[5]

Compared to randomization, developing matched control groups offers some significant advantages to researchers. It alleviates the need for working with the program administrator to encourage randomization, and rather than having to wait long periods for the implementation of randomized trials, in many cases, the researcher can make immediate use of post-adoption data. However, relative drawbacks include the need to understand a wide array of factors that encourage adoption, and the need to access data on those factors in the year(s) of adoption for both adopters and non-adopters. Furthermore, matching methods require the assumption that, besides those used by the researcher to create the matched groups, all *other* factors are randomly distributed across both the adopters and matched non-adopters.

Instrumental variable approaches

A third approach to avoiding selection bias is the "instrumental variables" technique. Although this approach avoids the challenges of convincing program administrators to randomize assignment and waiting long peri-

5 For more on matching techniques, Toffel (2006) provides a practical example of propensity score matching in his evaluation of the effects of the ISO 14001 Environmental Management System standard, and Smith and Todd (2005) provide excellent practical advice. For the conceptual and theoretical basis of matching techniques, see Heckman, Ichimura, and Todd 1998 and Rosenbaum and Rubin 1985.

ods for trials to be conducted, or of having to gather data on a wide array of factors that influence adoption, the challenges of this third technique are no less formidable. This approach requires identifying a variable with particularly unusual relationships to the other variables in the study. This special variable has to be correlated with adoption *and* have no direct influence on the performance variables once all other available factors are controlled for.[6] In effect, it has to approximate the features of random assignment.

It is often very difficult to identify appropriate instrumental variables. But we can illustrate the application to the study of the impact of voluntary codes with a hypothetical example. Imagine that the organization that oversees a particular code persuaded several major airline and hotel companies to distribute promotional fliers to their customers on a particular day to mark some relevant celebration or event (e.g., the 60th anniversary of the Universal Declaration of Human Rights). Suppose that managers of firms who read these fliers about the code are substantially more likely to adopt the code than counterparts who do not see the fliers. In this case, we could use whether managers of firms traveled on these airlines or stayed in these hotels on that particular day as an instrumental variable, modeling adoption of the code in a way that allows us to weed out selection-bias effects when conducting an analysis of performance measures among a sample of firms.

Conclusion

Although the research design criteria described in this chapter are not easy to implement, they are nonetheless standard practice in other domains of program evaluation. The number of organizations becoming certified under SA8000 and similar codes continues to rise, as additional codes governing working conditions continue to emerge. At the same time, a fierce debate is raging about whether these codes represent substantive efforts to improve working conditions or merely symbolic efforts

6 Technically, the instrumental variable has to be correlated with the adoption variable, but uncorrelated with the error term in the regression that predicts performance. The researcher can easily test the former, but the latter is an assumption that cannot be empirically proven (or disproven), and instead relies on the researcher making a compelling argument about why the assumption is plausible.

that allow organizations to score marketing points and counteract stakeholder pressure by merely filing some paperwork. Many critics have also raised questions about the skills and incentives of those charged with monitoring and certifying organizations as being in compliance with all the terms of these codes. Until more rigorous evaluations are conducted, these debates will continue unresolved. We believe evaluations designed with the features described in this chapter will help introduce systematic evidence to these important debates. This could help identify which particular codes are best able to distinguish those organizations with superior working conditions. Just as important, such evaluations might shed light on which elements of the codes are most effective and which types of monitoring systems represent best practices, and which areas are most in need of improvement.

References

Applebaum, Richard P. (2005) "Fighting Sweatshops: Problems of Enforcing Global Labor Standards," in Richard P. Applebaum and William I. Robinson (eds.), *Critical Global Studies* (New York: Routledge): 369-78.

Arnould, Eric J., Alejandro Plastina, and Dwayne Ball (2007) "Market Disintermediation and Producer Value Capture: The Case of Fair Trade Coffee in Nicaragua, Peru, and Guatemala," *Advances in International Management* 20: 319-40.

Barrientos, Stephanie, and Sally Smith (2006) *The ETI Code of Labour Practice: Do Workers Really Benefit?* (Brighton, UK: Institute of Development Studies, University of Sussex).

Becchetti, Leonardo, and Marco Constantino (2006) "The Effects of Fair Trade on Marginalised Producers: An Impact Analysis on Kenyan Farmers," Working Paper ECINEQ WP 2006-41, European Center for the Study of Income Inequality; www.ecineq.org/milano/WP/ECINEQ2006-41.pdf, accessed February 16, 2009.

Bennear, Lori S., and Cary Coglianese (2005) "Measuring Progress: Program Evaluation of Environmental Policies," *Environment* 47.2: 22-39.

Coglianese, Cary, Jennifer Nash, and Jonathan Borck (2008) "Evaluating the Social Effects of Performance-Based Environmental Programs," paper prepared for presentation at the conference *Dialogue on Performance-Based Environmental Programs: Better Ways to Measure and Communicate Results*, Harvard University Kennedy School of Government, Cambridge, MA, March 11, 2008; www.mswg.org/documents/PathtoWashington/Coglianese_Nash_Borck_Measuring%20Social%20EffectsFNL.pdf, accessed February 16, 2009.

Darnall, Nicole, and Stephen Sides (2008) "Assessing the Performance of Voluntary Environmental Programs: Does Certification Matter?" *Policy Studies Journal* 36.1: 95-117.

Ehrlich, Jennifer (2000) "Sweatshop Swindlers," *South China Morning Post*, December 18, 2000: 15.

Esbenshade, Jill (2004) *Monitoring Sweatshops: Workers, Consumers and the Global Apparel Industry* (Philadelphia, PA: Temple University Press).

Gilbert, Dirk Ulrich, and Andreas Rasche (2008) "A Critical Perspective on Social Accounting: The Contribution of Discourse Philosophy," in Christopher Cowton and Michaela Haase (eds.), *Trends in Business and Economic Ethics* (Berlin: Springer): 176-98.

Heckman, James J., Hidehiko Ichimura, and Petra Todd (1998) "Matching as an Econometric Evaluation Estimator," *Review of Economic Studies* 65.2: 261-94.

King, Andrew A., and Michael W. Toffel (2009) "Self-regulatory Institutions for Solving Environmental Problems: Perspectives and Contributions from the Management Literature," in Magali Delmas and Oran Young (eds.), *Government for the Environment: New Perspectives* (Cambridge, UK: Cambridge University Press).

Labour Rights in China (1999) *No Illusions: Against the Global Cosmetic SA 8000* (Hong Kong: Asia Monitor Resource Center).

Locke, Richard M., Thomas Kochan, Monica Romis, and Fei Qin (2007) "Beyond Corporate Codes of Conduct: Work Organization and Labour Standards at Nike's Suppliers," *International Labour Review* 146.1–2: 21-40.

—— and Monica Romis (2007) "Improving Work Conditions in a Global Supply Chain," *MIT Sloan Management Review* 48.2: 54-62.

——, Fei Qin, and Alberto Brause (2007) "Does Monitoring Improve Labor Standards? Lessons from Nike," *Industrial and Labor Relations Review* 61.1: 3-31.

Maquila Solidarity Network (2001) "Memo: Codes Update No. 8 (August)"; en.maquilasolidarity.org/en/node/531, accessed February 16, 2009.

Murray, Douglas L., Laura T. Raynolds, and Peter L. Taylor (2003) "One Cup at a Time: Poverty Alleviation and Fair Trade in Latin America," manuscript prepared for the Ford Foundation; www.colostate.edu/Depts/Sociology/FairTradeResearchGroup, accessed February 16, 2009.

——, Laura T. Raynolds, and Peter L. Taylor (2006) "The Future of Fair Trade Coffee: Dilemmas Facing Latin America's Small-Scale Producers," *Development in Practice* 16.2: 179-92.

Nelson, Valerie, Adrienne Martin, and Joachim Ewert (2007) "The Impacts of Codes of Practice on Worker Livelihoods: Empirical Evidence from the South African Wine and Kenyan Cut Flower Industries," *Journal of Corporate Citizenship* 28: 61-72.

O'Rourke, Dara (2000) "Monitoring the Monitors: A Critique of PricewaterhouseCooper's Labor Monitoring," Working Paper; nature.berkeley.edu/orourke, accessed February 16, 2009.

—— (2003) "Outsourcing Regulation: Analyzing Nongovernmental Systems of Labor Standards and Monitoring," *Policy Studies Journal* 31.1: 1-30.

Plastina, Alejandro, and Eric J. Arnould (2007) "Fair Trade Impacts on Educational Attainment and Health: A Three Country Comparison," White Paper 07-2001, Norton School, University of Arizona.

Raynolds, Laura T., Douglas Murray, and Peter L. Taylor (2004) "Fair Trade Coffee: Building Producer Capacity via Global Networks," *Journal of International Development* 16.8: 1,109-21.

Ronchi, Loraine (2002) "The Impact of Fair Trade on Producers and Their Organisations: A Case Study with Coocafé in Costa Rica," PRUS Working Paper No. 11. Poverty Research Unit at Sussex, University of Sussex; www.sussex.ac.uk/Units/PRU/wps/wp11.pdf, accessed February 16, 2009.

Rosenbaum, Paul R., and Donald B. Rubin (1985) "Constructing a Control Group Using Multivariate Matched Sampling Methods that Incorporate the Propensity Score," *American Statistician* 39.1: 33-38.

Smith, Jeffrey A., and Petra E. Todd (2005) "Does Matching Overcome Lalonde's Critique of Nonexperimental Estimators?" *Journal of Econometrics* 125.1–2: 305-53.

Toffel, Michael W. (2006) "Resolving Information Asymmetries in Markets: The Role of Certified Management Programs," Working Paper No. 07-023, Harvard Business School; www.hbs.edu/research/pdf/07-023.pdf, accessed February 16, 2009.

Vogel, David (2005) *The Market for Virtue: The Potential and Limits of Corporate Social Responsibility* (Washington, DC: Brookings Institution Press).

Weil, David, and Carlos Mallo (2007) "Regulating Labour Standards via Supply Chains: Combining Public/Private Interventions to Improve Workplace Compliance," *British Journal of Industrial Relations* 45.4: 791-814.

World Bank (2004) *Monitoring and Evaluation: Some Tools, Methods and Approaches* (Washington, DC: World Bank Operations Evaluation Department).

14

ISO 26000 and SA8000

Deborah Leipziger[1]
CSR consultant, United States

The International Organization for Standardization (ISO) is developing a voluntary set of guidelines on social responsibility that will be launched in 2010. Although these guidelines will not include a protocol for certification, they will provide guidance on core social responsibility issues, including:

- Organizational governance
- Environment
- Human rights (to include civil and political rights, economic rights, and fundamental rights at work)
- Labor practices
- Fair operating practices
- Consumer issues
- Community involvement and society development

1 This chapter is derived from an interview between Deborah Leipziger and Rochelle Zaid, Executive Director of SAAS, who serves as a D-Liaison to the ISO 26000 process.

ISO 26000 is designed to apply to all types of organization, whether they are small, medium, or large. Likewise, ISO 26000 can be used by companies, government agencies, or civil society organizations.

Organizations will be able to use the ISO 26000 Guidelines in many ways. First, the guidelines will provide a common language and framework for organizations. Second, organizations will be able to adopt the guidelines or use them to orient their own policies. Third, organizations can use the listing of issue areas to report on key topics.

Several countries are considering setting up national standards which could be used as certification standards. For example, both Portugal and Denmark are contemplating developing a standard for certification based on ISO 26000.

Differences between SA8000 and ISO 26000

There are significant differences between SA8000 and ISO 26000:

SA8000	ISO 26000
Certification standard	Guidance
Management systems	Descriptive
Labor issues, human rights	Environment, governance, human rights, labor practices, etc.
Multi-stakeholder	Multi-stakeholder, but with national committees

SA8000 is a standard that is certifiable, whereas ISO 26000 provides guidance to companies. SA8000 includes management systems, whereas ISO 26000 is descriptive. ISO 26000 covers a far broader range of issues than SA8000. While both ISO 26000 and SA8000 evolved through a multi-stakeholder process, ISO 26000 has a structure that involves national committees.

Controversial points in the debate on ISO 26000

It is useful to examine which issues were controversial in developing ISO 26000 as these relate to SA8000 in important ways.

1. Should companies be allowed to pick and choose issues or must they address all issues included within ISO 26000?
   - Companies must address all of the issues within ISO 26000. There can be no "cherry-picking" of issues
2. Should ISO 26000 include references to corporate social responsibility (CSR) standards such as SA8000?
   - There was contentious debate about the inclusion of standards such as SA8000 and guidelines such as the Global Reporting Initiative (GRI) within ISO 26000. While International Labour Organization (ILO) conventions are mentioned in the text along with ISO standards, SA8000 will not be referenced within the text of ISO 26000. SA8000 will be included in the annex of ISO 26000. One of the difficult issues the working group is grappling with is which initiatives are to be included in the annex and which criteria should be used to make the selection. Possible criteria for inclusion may include the following: the initiative must be international and in use by a significant number of organizations. Industry standards may also be included

How might ISO 26000 and SA8000 work synergistically?

Side-by-side report

Social Accountability International (SAI) will release a hard-copy document of SA8000 which demonstrates how SA8000 can help organizations to meet aspects of ISO 26000. Certification to SA8000 will demonstrate that a company complies with ISO 26000's labor rights and human rights and some aspects of provisions for fair operating practices, consumer issues, community involvement and development, and that there are management systems in place to ensure continuous improvement.

Reference point

The text of ISO 26000 will not reference other private initiatives such as SA8000 and the GRI. However, it is very likely that ISO 26000 will include annexes that refer to SA8000 and other social standards and private initiatives.

SAI provides training and consulting

The opportunity exists for SAI to provide significant training on how to implement SA8000 within the ISO 26000 model, as well as how current certification to SA8000 allows an organization to provide evidence that it has engaged with and is considering many elements of the ISO 26000 guidance.

The development of ISO 26000

ISO 26000 has developed through a series of international meetings where stakeholders from the groups listed below and D-liaison organizations participated in the initial drafting of the standard. Task groups and drafting groups were formed to develop the actual text. The working group of 300-plus members was responsible—along with input from mirror committees—to bring the standard through several drafts to a Committee Draft. At the Committee Draft level the national standards bodies will vote on the language. D-liaison organizations cannot vote but will have input through comments and through national committees. Representatives to the national committees come from several categories, including:

- Industry
- Trade unions
- Government
- Consumer groups
- Non-governmental organizations (NGOs)

The United States has a large delegation, with 40 people serving on the national committee from many different sectors and representing many different interests. Not all national committees are multi-stakeholder. Nor can all countries afford to send representatives. In addition to the national committees, experts or D-liaisons are also invited to participate, including representatives from the GRI, SAI, AccountAbility, Transparency International, and the UN Global Compact. D-liaisons can make comments but not vote. They can, however, try to influence their national delegation.

Each country participating develops a mirror committee made up of individuals from each stakeholder group (where possible). The mirror committee's role during this process is to feed back comments and positions to be shared with the entire working group as well as with their stakeholder group representatives throughout the commenting period. The review process has been quite extensive, with comments received from 7,000 organizations and individuals.

Evaluating ISO 26000

There are many ways in which ISO 26000 can be evaluated. One of the key questions to address is whether ISO 26000 creates something new. ISO 26000 has created new alliances. For example, there are Memoranda of Understanding between ISO 26000 and:

- The Global Compact
- The International Labour Organization
- The Global Reporting Initiative

ISO 26000 has been a breakthrough in making the ISO process more reliant on a multi-stakeholder process.

The future of ISO 26000

It is possible that ISO 26000 will become a certification standard eventually, rather than a guidance standard as is planned for 2010. There are a number of countries that do not want to wait for ISO 26000 to become a certification standard. Portugal is the first country to set up a certifiable standard around ISO 26000 for Portugal. It is possible that Social Accountability Accreditation Services (SAAS) could accredit the system.

There are several issues that need to be considered around accreditation. First, it is not clear that there is market demand for certification around ISO 26000. Second, national accreditation does not address the issue of global supply chains.

There are several scenarios that may emerge:

- **Scenario 1.** Certification bodies such as SGS and Bureau Veritas Certification (formerly BVQI) might develop their own model to show compliance. This could include a gap analysis and auditable provisions. This is possible, but difficult to achieve because ISO 26000 is very broad in scope
- **Scenario 2.** Develop a system which shows how different models (e.g. GRI and SA8000) work within the ISO 26000 framework
- **Scenario 3.** In alliance with national bodies, SAAS accredits certification bodies. However, this depends on the laws in different countries. There is a precedent for an ISO guidance tool that becomes a certification standard
- **Scenario 4.** ISO 26000 may evolve sector standards which are certifiable and based on management systems

Will ISO 26000 be useful?

The extent to which ISO 26000 will be useful will depend on several factors, including the ability of the drafting committee to eliminate jargon and make the document accessible. If the final document is written as simply as possible, then it will be useful.

Demand from developing countries for ISO 26000 is growing. It is unlikely that there will be significant levels of demand for ISO 26000 within the U.S. corporate structure, according to Dr. Bradley Googins of the Boston College's Center for Corporate Citizenship.[2]

Reference

Slob, Bart, and Gerard Oonk (2007) *ISO Working Group on Social Responsibility: Developing the Future ISO SR 26000*, Standard, Briefing Paper; inni.pacinst.org/inni/corporate_social_responsibility/ISOSRWGBriefingPaperEn.pdf, accessed April 20, 2009.

2 Interview between Deborah Leipziger and Dr. Bradley Googins, October 21, 2008.

15

The impact of SA8000 in Brazil

Beat Grüninger
BSD Consulting, Brazil

In the last decade, Brazil has transformed itself into a leader among emerging markets in the field of corporate social responsibility (CSR). The impressive growth of interest in CSR and in sustainability on the part of companies and consumers is a result of the tireless work of the Ethos Institute, a business-led non-governmental organization (NGO) promoting CSR practices in Brazil. Supported by Ethos and after a timid start, SA8000 certification reached a turning point when strong market players such as Petrobras entered the scene. Today, SA8000 has shown proven positive impacts in a wide range of sectors and is integrated in the most important national CSR tools such as the Ethos Indicators and the Index of Sustainable Enterprises of the Brazilian Stock Exchange, Bovespa.

SAI and Ethos: a common history

SA8000 and the Ethos Institute have several aspects in common: both originated from a deep concern with unfair labor conditions. Ethos has its primary origin in the fight against child labor. Both Social Accountability International (SAI) and Ethos have shown solid and sustainable growth over the last decade, thanks to the engagement of some leading companies adhering to the standard and adopting the principles that Ethos is promoting via its own effective tools.

It was in the early 1990s that leading entrepreneurs of the toy industry, under the guidance of Oded Grajew, founder of Ethos, convened to establish an organization that focused on a direct link between consumers and the promotion of better conditions for Brazilian children. Having mobilized the private sector and civil society to approve the Brazilian Statue of Children's Rights in 1990, the Abrinq Foundation[1] launched what was later to become the first and probably most successful product label in Brazil, the label for "child-friendly" enterprises. Under this program, Empresa Amiga da Criança (Child-Friendly Company), companies had to sign a commitment to work actively against child labor in their sphere of influence and support social projects benefiting youth and children. The commitment and financial support of the Foundation allowed them to label their products and company communications with the specific label that is still in use today.

The Abrinq Foundation's ground-breaking work led to the foundation of the Ethos Institute, which allowed Oded Grajew and other leaders to widen the understanding of companies' accountability and influence management introducing CSR practices. One of the strategies of Ethos was to support emerging social standards, and Ethos has been—together with other Brazilian NGOs such as the Brazilian Institute for Social and Economic Analysis (IBASE)—essential for the introduction of SA8000 in Brazil. Oded Grajew was from the beginning an active supporter of initiative of the Council on Economic Priorities (CEP) and currently he and the president of Akatu Institute, an organization that is working on consumer awareness for sustainability issues, serve as alternates on the Advisory Board of SAI. SAI's president, Alice Tepper Marlin, also serves on the Ethos International Council.

A slow start—but solid growth

The Abrinq label has been very effective and also turned out to have a positive impact for user companies internally by motivating employee

1 Abrinq (Associação Brasileira de Fabricantes de Brinquedos—Brazilian Association of Toy Makers) is the name of the sectoral association.

satisfaction (Fischer and Falconer 2002).[2] But ,even if Abrinq's Child-Friendly label has been adopted quickly by major economic players (the number of label users rose in the first five years to 1,346 companies in 1999) (Fischer and Falconer 2002: 64), the step to a more rigid approach of certification was meeting more resistance. The Abrinq program did not foresee any external verification of working conditions or child labor policies, and the organization had to revise its self-commitment approach at a later stage to prevent credibility risk, introducing a ten-step approach and documented proof of progress and management practices.

The Council on Economic Priorities Accreditation Agency (CEPAA) held a first consultation workshop on SA8000 in June 1999, bringing together the major stakeholders to present, discuss, and promote the standard. Nevertheless, the start of SA8000 was timid and by 2002, fewer than ten companies had been certified: Avon and its supplier Cosmotec, the food company De Nadai, AFL (an Alcoa asset in the automotive industry), CESG (a consultancy), Bahia Sul Celulose and the first SA-certified agri-business, Santa Elisa, a sugar and alcohol factory. The slow start may have had to do with the fact that Brazil has very complex and strong labor legislation, Consolidação das Leis do Trabalho (CLT Consolidated Labor Legislation), which provides workers in the most important industrial and services sectors with strong benefits and rights. Along with this, trade unions are mandatory and receive financial support from the federal government. This allows them to maintain strong organizations within all sectors and in all geographical contexts.

Even if the legal context is impressive, the reality for many workers is far from comfortable, especially in the rural sector and the informal businesses that form part of the supply chains of big companies and multinationals. The demands of the export market, the growing awareness of consumers created by Ethos, IBASE, and specialist news agencies such as ANDI and Reporter Brasil,[3] as well as the conviction that there is a big gap between laws and their enforcement, nurtured the necessity in many companies to introduce a solid system that proved—especially to foreign buyers—that they were respecting collective bargaining agreements and human rights. Leading companies that had already gone through a strong quality-improvement phase soon analyzed the advantages that certifica-

2 A discussion paper published by the University of São Paulo (USP), based on impact research carried out in 1999 and 2000.

3 Two important news agencies that denounce slave and child labor conditions.

tion could bring, and the first positive impact reports from the first users stimulated them to go ahead.[4]

At the same time, a major event in the development of SA8000 was the decision of Petrobras, Brazil's state-owned oil company and, with more than 70,000 staff, the largest company in South America, to adopt the standard for several of its assets. Since the standards criteria prohibit the certification of extractive activities on oil platforms, only industrial units such as refineries have been certified. Due to the restrictions, the company could not declare SA8000 as a company-wide social standard. If Petrobras had done this, the impact would have been even more significant than it was, because in a few years the number of certified companies grew to more than 90 and Brazil reached third place in the worldwide ranking of certified facilities.

FIGURE 15.1 Overview of certified facilities in Brazil (by sector)

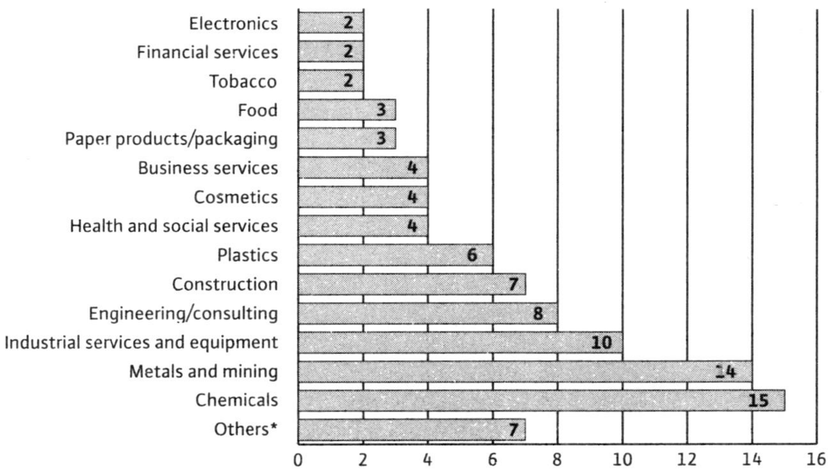

* Others include: Automotive, Cleaning services, Waste management, Logistics, Furnishing, Footwear, Energy

Recently, the financial sector has also become interested in certification, with the banks Bradesco and HSBC Brasil among the first financial

4 Santa Elisa reported a 34% production increase to 12% reduction of absenteeism after certification.

institutions to get SA8000 certification. Another bank, Itaú, is taking steps towards certification. Other specific sectors that have sought certification in an innovative way are legislative bodies including the parliament of the city of Barueri in greater São Paulo, the Sabin Health Laboratory, and the 6º Oficio de Registro de Titulos e Documentos, an official legal registering office, all pioneers in their sector of business.

It is worth mentioning that many of the certified facilities are medium-sized companies[5] which are suppliers to certified multinationals or linked to the export business. Unfortunately, agri-business, which shows the greatest risk and deficits in guaranteeing labor rights, is still less developed than other sectors, but the growing worldwide interest in sugar-based ethanol as a fuel has led several industries linked to this sector to start implementation procedures.

Major achievements and challenges

The impacts of SA8000 certification on a company level have not been systematically researched and consolidated yet, but individual case studies[6] make clear that certified companies have experienced positive impacts of the process immediately after certification. A major problem for Brazilian companies is the issue of working hours; due to relatively low liquid salaries (more than 60% of salaries are benefits), on the one hand workers tend to accept extra hours as a way of earning more money, and on the other hand middle management and administrative staff often work more than the legally allowed 44 hours. With respect to working hours, companies that implemented a management system succeeded in reducing extra hours, saving costs and even enhancing productivity and employee satisfaction. Soon after certification, companies are reporting a reduction of working hours, lower rates of absenteeism, and better health and safety rates.

Brazilian companies reported the following benefits of certification:

5 According to Sebrae, the Brazilian Support Service for Small and Medium Enterprises, at least one in three of the certified companies are small and medium enterprises (SMEs).

6 Guillardi 2006 and internal data of BSD Consulting, São Paulo.

- Massive reduction in extra hours
- Increase in productivity
- Higher levels of staff satisfaction
- Reduction in absenteeism
- Reduction in labor rights law suits
- Reduction in child labor risks in the supply chain
- Better turnover rates
- Reduction of accident rates
- Enhanced reputation
- Compliance advantages in contracting
- Better insurance rates
- Assurance against child labor in the supply chain

In certain cases, SA-related processes led to changes in management approaches to discrimination and disciplinary practices, even if these are not major issues for the Brazilian working reality. No major changes have been observed in trade union relations, as the position of Brazilian trade unions towards SA8000 is unclear. Unlike in other countries, trade unions in Brazil are not strongly engaged in SA8000 even if Instituto Observatório Social, a labor relations research and monitoring institution linked to the Central Trade Unions (CUT), presents the standard in its publication and its website (Instituto Observatório Social 2004). One major problem is that trade unions sometimes consider the SA worker-representative as a competitor and therefore undermine election processes. It is important that trade unions gain more awareness about the advantages of certification and that a stronger link between SAI and unions be established in the future.

Another ongoing challenge for Brazilian companies is the social gap in the supply chain. Sophisticated processing industries that meet the highest quality and safety standards are still confronting a very different reality in the small and medium companies that are part of the subcontracting chain. Agri-business, the apparel industry, construction and the steel sector maybe the most critical areas: detection of slave and child labor in urban and rural areas by the Public Ministry of Labor is common in Brazil. The daily news exposés of Bolivian immigrant workers in sweatshops in São Paulo's Brás district or children working with their parents in charcoal production for the steel industry in the state of Pará are as common as TV reports on the liberation of bonded workers in large farms in remote areas.

Brazil has a minimum age of 16 for child labor. According to the Brazilian Statistics Institute IBGE, around 3 million children up to 15 years of age were working in 2006, 53.4% of them in the agricultural sector. The number has reduced only slightly since the beginning of this century and it is still a major concern for companies that want to work with Brazilian suppliers. Eliminating child and slave labor will be an ongoing task for government agencies and companies, which have to strengthen massively their control of the supply chain. Control of suppliers is one of the major challenges that SA8000 management systems have to address in Brazil, but new initiatives and CSR tools may help to make progress on this issue in the coming years.

The interface between SA8000 and local tools

One of the major results of SA8000 in Brazil is not only that it reaches out to companies in many different sectors and of different sizes, but also that it succeeds in integrating with other major initiatives in the national CSR landscape. Hundreds of companies in Brazil use the Ethos Indicators, a set of 40 scaled indicators, to measure their performance and compare to benchmarks in the sector and the country on an annual basis. The Indicators are structured in seven areas, two of which—covering staff and supplier relations—have direct links to SA8000. All SA8000 criteria have been fully integrated into the tool. Companies that use SA management systems have naturally a better score than other companies without specific management processes of labor relations. The application of the Indicators led many companies to the decision to adopt certification, in order to formalize policies and processes necessary to advance in their evaluation.

A second important move was the introduction of SA-related items in the Index of Sustainable Enterprises of the Brazilian Stock Exchange Bovespa, known as the ISE ranking. The ISE was created in 2005 and boasts a very positive performance. Under the 30 companies classified for the Index in 2007 we find several SA8000-certified companies such as Bradesco, Petrobras, Suzano, and CPFL. Table 15.1 shows the interface between SA8000 criteria and ISE Ranking and Ethos Indicators. SA8000 certification has become an important asset also for the risk evaluation of financial institutions. Banks such as ABN Amro Real use SA8000 as a reference in their risk evaluation, which constitutes part of their practical application of the Equator Principles.

TABLE 15.1 Interface between SA8000 and local tools

SA8000 criteria	Ethos Indicators	Bovespa Sustainability Index (ISE)
• Child labor • Forced labor • Discrimination • Working hours • Disciplinary practices • Compensation • Collective bargaining • Health and safety • Management systems	All items addressed in the sections: • Staff relations • Supplier management	Items addressed in the social dimensions under the following items: • Basic labor rights, policy and management • Staff relations • Supplier relations • Society • Diversity

Another important factor for the future growth of SA8000 is the fact that Brazil is a leading nation in publishing sustainability reports which are based on the Guidelines for Sustainability Reporting of the Global Reporting Initiative (GRI). Companies that are SA8000-certified already have a management system which allows them to report labor and human rights indicators completely and on a solid and externally audited data basis. Over 70 major companies in Brazil report against GRI indicators and the number is increasing rapidly.

A specific element that is preventing a faster integration of SA8000 might be due to the fact that Brazil has— under the leadership of Ethos and the Brazilian Standard Association (ABNT)—elaborated its own social norm ABNT16000. ABNT16000 has a much wider scope, including all stakeholders relations and issues, but it has not reached a breakthrough in Brazil. Nevertheless, it paved the way for Brazilian leadership in the ISO 26000 guidelines elaboration process. Brazil is, with Sweden, chair of the Working Group, a fact that drew the attention of local companies to this new standard elaboration process. But, observing in which direction they should go, companies ended up deciding to introduce SA8000 in order to provide a clearly defined social component to their integrated management system.

Expansion in the rural sector

The current developments on the world's energy market, which tends to focus on renewable bio-energy such as Brazilian ethanol derived from sugar cane, may have a significant impact on the future development of SA8000 in Brazil. It is very probable that a great number of factories in this industry, which contracts thousands of rural workers, will work with the SA8000-standard. Several governments in the Northern Hemisphere have already introduced social clauses for bio-fuels and consumer organizations and NGOs are watching with great interest the developments in this field.

Social clauses in international trade, internal pressure from trade unions, reporting requirements, and the incentives of the financial sector will surely strengthen the Brazilian industry's pursuit of solid social management systems. It is foreseeable that Brazil will maintain its position as a leading nation for CSR development within the emerging markets.

References

Fischer, Rosa Maria, and Andrés Falconer (2002) "O selo social contra o trabalho infantil: Experiências brasileiras" (discussion paper; São Paulo: CEATS–University of São Paulo/OIT [Organização Internacional de Trabalho; ILO]).

Guillardi, Catia Roberta (2006) "Certificação social: Um estudo sobre os benefícios da norma SA8000 em empresas certificadas," São Caetano Do Sul: Universidade Municipal De São Caetano Do Sul; www.ead.fea.usp.br/semead/9semead/resultado_semead/an_resumo.asp?cod_trabalho=76, accessed April 20, 2009.

Instituto Observatório Social (2004) *Responsabilidade Social Empresarial. Persepctivas para atuação sindical* (Florianópolis, Brazil: Instituto Observatório Social; www.observatoriosocial.org.br).

About the contributors

Lorenz Berzau grew up in Germany and Belgium. He studied law in Göttingen and Bonn with a focus on economic and administrative law, finalizing his legal education with the second state examination in 2002. He then joined the Foreign Trade Association of the German Retail Trade (AVE) in Cologne where he was project coordinator of the AVE Sector Model Social Responsibility. He was involved in the launch of the Business Social Compliance Initiative (BSCI), and since 2004 has coordinated the BSCI at the Brussels-based Foreign Trade Association (FTA).

Franco Furnò is the Worldwide Director of Human Resources at Gucci. After earning a degree in Sociology at Trento University and a master's degree at the London School of Economics and Political Science, his career began in 1981 at Zanussi. In 1983 he joined the Benetton Group, where he occupied various positions and was finally appointed Director of Human Resources. In 1993, he was appointed Central Director of Organizational Development at Marzotto. In 1995, a desire for international experience brought him to London to work for the European Bank for Reconstruction and Development where he served as Director of Human Resources for eight years. On returning to Italy in 2003, he took up the role of Director of Human Resources for the PAM Group. At the end of 2004 he joined Gucci.

Beat Grüninger is the co-founder of BSD Consulting (www.bsd-net.com) and has led the BSD office in Brazil since 1998. Beat has a bachelor's degree in French Literature, Linguistics, and Communications from the University of Zurich, and a postgraduate degree in Cooperation for Development from the Swiss Federal Institute of Technology (ETH) in Zurich. He previously worked as a journalist and as a communications officer in the Swiss Committee for UNICEF. He is a trained consultant in Accountability Standard AA1000 by SGS/EQManagement/Forum for the Future, a certified Associate Sustainability Assurance Practitioner registered at the International Register of Certified Auditors, and is an auditor for SA8000. He lectures on social norms at the Fundação Getúlio Vargas Business School in São Paulo and currently acts as Project Manager of the Responsible Sourcing Partnership, a project of TransFair USA, USAID, Café Bom Dia and Wal-Mart, which focuses on market access and production quality of 5,000 Brazilian Fair Trade-certified coffee producers.

Dan Henkle is Gap Inc.'s Senior Vice President of Global Responsibility. He heads a team of more than 120 employees worldwide responsible for the company's global responsibility efforts. His team includes ethical sourcing, environmental affairs, employee relations, social and community investment, diversity and inclusion, learning and development, and global partnerships. He joined the company in 1992 and served as the Vice President of Human Resources for the Gap division before joining the Social Responsibility team. Prior to joining Gap Inc., he worked in the human resources function for Oracle Corporation. He received a BSc in accounting and general management from Purdue University, and his MBA with an emphasis on organizational behavior from the Haas School of Business at the University of California, Berkeley. He currently serves on the Board of Directors of Social Accountability International, a multi-stakeholder organization focused on improving conditions in workplaces throughout the world.

Michael J. Hiscox is Professor of Government in the Department of Government at Harvard University. He has published widely in the areas of international political economy and international relations. His research focuses on the politics of international trade, investment, immigration, and globalization. He teaches in the Department of Government and in the Social Studies program at Harvard and is a faculty associate at the Weatherhead Center for International Affairs and at the Institute for Quantitative Social Science.

Mark Huis in't Veld has been the managing director of MADE-BY since its inception in 2004. He has worked for 20 years in marketing and communication of sustainable products for companies such as Triodos Bank, Fair Trade Original, and fair trade label Max Havelaar.

George Jaksch is the Senior Director of Corporate Responsibility and Public Affairs at Chiquita's European headquarters in Antwerp, Belgium. In his 20 years with Chiquita he has worked in banana production in Latin America and Africa, and in various management functions in the United States and Europe. He is a member of Chiquita's corporate responsibility steering committee, of Social Accountability International's advisory board, and of the labor advisory group of the International Finance Corporation.

A graduate of Wellesley College, where she earned a BA in Economics, **Eileen Kohl Kaufman** also holds an MA in Economics and an MBA in Finance from Columbia University. Ms. Kaufman has contributed to various publications including *ISO Management Systems*, *Aid & Trade Review*, *Enterprise Ethique*, *Business & Society Review*, and *Business and Human Rights Dilemmas and Solutions*. She has been with Social Accountability International (SAI) since it was incorporated in May 1997. Prior to joining SAI, she worked at the New York City Departments of Environmental Protection, Design and Construction, and the NYC Water Board. At the organization's inception, she worked at the Council on Economic Priorities, co-authoring *Paper Profits*, an analysis of paper mill pollution and its control by the 24 largest U.S. paper manufacturers.

Deborah Leipziger is an author and consultant in the field of CSR. She is the author of *The Corporate Responsibility Code Book* (Greenleaf Publishing, 2003), among other volumes on CSR. She advises companies, UN agencies, governments, and NGOs on CSR issues.

Martin Ma joined Social Accountability International in January 2001, being involved with research and guidance in the revision of SA8000. Martin moved back to China in 2004, to develop programs on the ground, including worker training, a capacity-building project for internal compliance teams, and public education on issues related to sustainability. As of March 2006, Martin has been managing programs for Solidaridad, a Netherlands-based NGO focusing on development aid. Solidaridad's major task in China is to offer assistance to local actors, farmers, workers, and businesses, to build a new model of business promoting ecological, social, and economical development.

Janet Mensink is the Coordinator Sustainable Fashion Program at Solidaridad, a Dutch NGO. She holds an MSc in Environmental Science from Wageningen University. She has worked at the Dutch consultancy CREM (Consultancy and Research for Environmental Management) and is a specialist on sustainable textiles.

Dr. **Johannes Merck** is Vice President Corporate Responsibility at the Otto Group (Hamburg). He took his degree in history and law at the Free University Berlin (PhD 1990). After working for the German Parliament (Bundestag) from 1986 to 1989, he joined the Otto Group in 1989. His fields of expertise are corporate social responsibility, foundation management, and consulting.

Craig Moss is the Director of Corporate Programs and Training at Social Accountability International (SAI). Mr. Moss develops and manages programs to assist companies with continuous improvements in their supply chain. As Director of Training, he oversees SAI training for auditors, suppliers, and buyers on social compliance in the supply chain and SA8000. Prior to joining SAI, Mr. Moss worked extensively in international business development, focusing on export development and investment attraction for emerging market companies and governments. He is a graduate of Hampshire College.

Stefania Orselli is the Industrial Relations Manager at Gucci. After completing a degree in Political Sciences specializing in Labor Law at Pisa University and a master's degree at Florence University in Human Resources Administration, her career began in Superal—at that time part of the German large-scale retail trade corporation Tengelmann—where she served as HR Manager. In 2001 she joined Gilbarco S.p.A, where she was appointed Human Resources Manager. Gilbarco is a leading American company producing automation systems for controlling and administrating service stations. In 2003 she joined Gucci where she was HR Manager for the Sergio Rossi brand, a company of the Gucci Group. During her experience at Gucci she has worked closely with Franco Furnò on implementing the CSR project leading to the SA8000 certification.

Mike Patrick is the Global Director of Corporate Responsibility at TNT Express and is based in the UK and the Netherlands. He is responsible for the development and implementation of the global strategies for corporate social responsibility. Mike joined TNT Express in 2002 in the health, safety, and environmental department in Amsterdam and has held various positions over the last five years within the divisional head office. Prior to his current position, Mike was responsible for environment, ISO, and OHSAS Standards, and sustainability and environmental stewardship programs globally. Mike is a qualified engineer and has worked in manufacturing, enforcement, training, human resources, risk management, and operations in the public and private sectors.

Paloma Raggo is currently a PhD candidate in Political Science at the Maxwell School of Citizenship and Public Affairs of Syracuse University. Her past research is focused on transnational NGOs, non-governmental systems of governance, and issues of accountability.

Claire A. Schwartz is a PhD candidate in the Department of Government at Harvard University, a graduate student associate of the Weatherhead Center for International Affairs, and a fellow with the Project on Justice, Welfare, and Economics. Her research focuses on international political economy, and her dissertation explores the interaction between private and public governance against the backdrop of globalization.

Priyadarshini Sharma, Senior Manager at Tata Steel working on business excellence and sustainability aspects, is convener of the SA8000 Management Review Committee. She joined the Tata Group centralized personnel cadre, the Tata Administrative Service (TAS), and through it Tata Steel. She holds masters' degrees in Communication Studies and Public Administration. During the course of her studies in the United States, she worked with Metropolitan Atlanta Rapid Transit Authority (MARTA), with the 1996 Summer Olympic Games, and on quality consulting with the Fulton County School District (Atlanta). Her postgraduate projects have been with a U.S. House of Representatives Subcommittee (Washington, DC) and the Atlanta-Fulton County Emergency Management Agency with the aim to bring back specialized learning to her country, India.

Michael W. Toffel is an Assistant Professor at the Harvard Business School, a Faculty Fellow at the Harvard Environmental Economics Program, and a Faculty Affiliate at the Kennedy School of Government's Regulatory Policy Program. His research examines codes of conduct and management standards governing environmental and occupational safety issues, using methods ranging from econometric analyses of large datasets to case studies of individual companies. He also examines how companies disclose information about their environmental and labor practices to buyers, regulators, and other stakeholders.

Morton Winston is Professor of Philosophy and Chairman of the Department of Philosophy and Religion at The College of New Jersey. His areas of specialization include human rights theory and practice, biomedical ethics, political philosophy, and philosophy of technology. His most recent books are *On Chomsky* (Wadsworth, 2001) and *Society, Ethics, and Technology* (Wadsworth, 2009). In addition to his academic career, Dr. Winston has had a career as a human rights activist. He served as chairman of Amnesty International USA (AIUSA)'s national board of directors from 1995 to 1997 and was named honorary chair of AIUSA in 2003. He has been a member of the Advisory Board of Social Accountability International since 1999. Prof. Winston has received three Fulbright Scholarships: to South Africa in 1992, to Thailand in 1999, and in 2007 he held the Danish Distinguished Chair of Human Rights and International Relations at the Danish Institute of Human Rights in Copenhagen. Dr. Winston attended Swarthmore College, graduating with High Honors and Phi Beta Kappa. He received his MA in cognitive psychology and PhD in philosophy from the University of Illinois at Urbana–Champaign.

Index

NOTE: Page numbers in *italic figures* refer to figures and tables